From Stonehenge to Skylines

Ancient Isles and Early Inhabitants: Tracing the Origins of the United Kingdom

The history of the United Kingdom is deeply rooted in the ancient past, with a tapestry woven from the threads of countless civilizations, migrations, and interactions. Stretching back millennia, the story of these lands begins with the earliest human inhabitants who left their indelible mark on the landscape and culture.

Archaeological evidence tells us that humans have inhabited the British Isles for hundreds of thousands of years. During the Paleolithic era, hunter-gatherer communities roamed these lands, leaving behind tools and artifacts that offer us tantalizing glimpses into their daily lives. As the Ice Age receded, the landscape transformed, and early inhabitants adapted to these changing conditions.

Around 4,500 BCE, the Neolithic Revolution brought significant shifts. Communities began to practice agriculture, transitioning from a nomadic lifestyle to settled farming. Evidence of this period can be seen in the construction of ancient monuments like Stonehenge, a testament to the engineering prowess and spiritual beliefs of these early people.

Fast forward to around 2,000 BCE, and the Bronze Age arrives, marked by technological advancements in metalworking. Burial sites and ceremonial centers from this era reveal the social and religious structures that were developing. The introduction of metal tools and weapons transformed everyday life, trade, and warfare.

But the history of the British Isles was far from isolated. The Celts, a collection of tribes with shared linguistic and cultural elements, began migrating from Central Europe around 500 BCE. They brought with them their distinctive languages and intricate artistry, shaping the landscape with hillforts and settlements. Their influence would later resonate in the folklore and traditions of the United Kingdom.

The Roman invasion of Britain in 43 CE brought about a new era of contact and transformation. The Romans established control over parts of the island, building roads, cities like Londinium (modern-day London), and Hadrian's Wall to mark the northern boundary of their empire. This period of occupation introduced urbanization, governance, and technological advancements, leaving a lasting imprint on the cultural fabric.

As the Roman Empire declined, the legions withdrew from Britain in the early 5th century, opening the door for the next wave of historical actors: the Anglo-Saxons. Germanic tribes from the continent migrated to the British Isles, establishing several distinct kingdoms. Their language and social structures would lay the groundwork for the English language and the foundation of England itself.

However, the Anglo-Saxon kingdoms faced incursions from the Norsemen, commonly known as Vikings, starting in the 8th century. These Scandinavian seafarers brought their own culture, trade networks, and settlements, leaving an impact that extended beyond their raiding reputation.

Their influence reached deep into English society, as seen in place names, legal codes, and even genetic markers.

As the medieval period approached, the landscape of the British Isles continued to evolve. The Kingdom of England began to take shape under the rule of various Anglo-Saxon and Norman kings, leading to the Norman Conquest of 1066 and the subsequent amalgamation of Norman and Anglo-Saxon cultures. The feudal system established during this time would shape societal structures for centuries to come.

Celtic Legacies and Roman Conquests: The Land Before England

In the shadows of prehistory, the British Isles were a canvas on which the early Celtic cultures painted their legacy. The enigmatic landmass, shrouded in mist and myth, witnessed the rise of Celtic tribes that would infuse the region with a rich tapestry of traditions, languages, and beliefs.

The Celts, an Indo-European people, began their migratory journey from the continent around 500 BCE. With them, they brought distinct languages, artistry, and a strong sense of community. The influence of Celtic culture resonated in every corner of the British Isles, shaping the very landscape they inhabited. One of the most striking remnants of this era is the Celtic hillforts. These fortified settlements, constructed on prominent hills and ridges, served as centers of political, social, and economic activity. Iron Age Celts displayed remarkable engineering skills, building intricate earthworks and ramparts that stand testament to their strategic acumen.

The intricate artistry of the Celts is perhaps best exemplified by their metalwork. Elaborate gold torcs, intricate jewelry, and finely crafted weapons showcase their mastery of intricate designs and skilled craftsmanship. Their penchant for abstraction and intricate patterns found their way into everyday objects, transforming the mundane into objects of beauty. But Celtic culture was not confined to the material realm alone. Druids, the revered class of religious leaders and scholars, held a prominent place within society. These individuals played the dual role of spiritual guides and keepers of oral tradition. Celtic mythology, a blend of nature reverence and deities, was passed down through generations, leaving behind a rich tapestry of legends that still intrigue us today.

However, the rise of the Roman Empire cast a shadow over the Celtic way of life. In 43 CE, Roman legions, led by Emperor Claudius, launched an invasion of Britain. The Romans, drawn by the island's resources and strategic value, established control over southeastern Britain, and eventually expanded their influence further north.

Romanization brought significant changes to the region. Major cities like Londinium (London) were founded as centers of administration, trade, and culture. Roman engineering feats such as roads and aqueducts crisscrossed the landscape, shaping the infrastructure of the British Isles for centuries to come.

The Roman presence introduced urbanization, written language, and a complex system of governance. Roman law, architecture, and artistry left their marks, merging with local traditions to create a unique fusion of cultures. The hypocaust heating systems in villas, intricate mosaics, and monumental structures stood as physical testaments to Roman ingenuity.

But the Roman-British relationship was not without its tensions. The resistance led by Boudicca, the Queen of the Iceni tribe, against Roman rule in the 1st century CE, stands as an example of the conflicts that arose from this cultural collision. Boudicca's rebellion highlighted the fierce determination of the Celtic tribes to defend their lands and way of life.

Anglo-Saxon Ascendance: Shaping the Foundations of a Kingdom

With the departure of the Roman legions in the early 5th century CE, the British Isles entered a period of transition marked by the arrival of the Anglo-Saxons. These Germanic tribes, hailing from modern-day Denmark, Germany, and the Netherlands, embarked on a migration that would lay the foundations for the future Kingdom of England.

The Anglo-Saxon influx brought a complex blend of cultures and languages to the region. The indigenous Celtic tribes found themselves faced with a significant challenge as they encountered the newcomers. The Anglo-Saxons established several distinct kingdoms, each with its own rulers, laws, and societal structures.

The era's history is illuminated by the writings of historians like Bede, whose "Historia Ecclesiastica Gentis Anglorum" provides insights into the early Anglo-Saxon period. Bede's chronicles reveal the intricacies of political power struggles, alliances, and the emergence of warrior elites.

The Anglo-Saxon kingdoms were characterized by their adherence to Germanic traditions, where kinship and allegiance were paramount. Society was divided into various classes, with the king or chieftain at the top, followed by the warrior elite, freemen, and slaves. Land ownership played a central role in defining social status and wealth.

One of the most defining aspects of this era was the Anglo-Saxon legal codes. King Æthelberht of Kent is renowned for establishing one of the earliest written legal codes in the 6th century. Known as the "Laws of Æthelberht," these codes outlined various aspects of justice, including penalties for crimes and the payment of wergild, a form of compensation for injuries or deaths.

As Christianity gained a foothold in the region, the Anglo-Saxons experienced a significant shift in their religious beliefs. The arrival of Augustine of Canterbury in 597 CE marked the beginning of a concerted effort to convert the Anglo-Saxon kingdoms to Christianity. This religious transformation not only brought about changes in spiritual beliefs but also served to unify various kingdoms under a shared faith.

The Anglo-Saxons were skilled artisans, as evidenced by their intricate metalwork, illuminated manuscripts, and jewelry. The Lindisfarne Gospels and the Sutton Hoo burial site offer glimpses into their craftsmanship and artistic prowess. The fusion of Christian themes with Germanic artistry in illuminated manuscripts showcases the syncretic nature of their culture.

However, the Anglo-Saxon kingdoms were not isolated entities. Viking raids from the 8th to the 11th centuries punctuated this period. Norse raiders, drawn by the riches of the Anglo-Saxon kingdoms, left a lasting impact on society, economy, and culture. The Danelaw, a region under Norse control in the north and east of England, reflects the intricate interactions between Anglo-Saxons and Vikings.

The Anglo-Saxon period also witnessed the emergence of a distinctive Old English language. This language, a fusion of Anglo-Saxon, Norse, and Celtic influences, laid the groundwork for the evolution of the English language we know today. Literary works like "Beowulf," an epic poem that draws on heroic themes and pagan legends, exemplify the linguistic and cultural complexities of the time.

The 10th century marked a significant turning point with the eventual unification of England under the Wessex dynasty. King Æthelstan, often referred to as the "First King of England," established a centralized monarchy and paved the way for a more cohesive realm. This pivotal moment set the stage for the transition from the Anglo-Saxon period to the subsequent Norman Conquest, heralding yet another chapter in the multifaceted history of the British Isles.

Viking Raiders and Danelaw: The Kingdoms Under Norse Influence

In the annals of history, the Viking Age stands as a tumultuous era that brought about significant changes to the British Isles. The seafaring Norsemen, hailing from modern-day Scandinavia, embarked on raids and conquests that reshaped the political, social, and cultural landscape of the region.

The Vikings, renowned for their mastery of shipbuilding and navigation, struck fear into the hearts of coastal communities as they arrived in their iconic longships. Their raids, beginning in the late 8th century, targeted monasteries, towns, and settlements, leaving destruction in their wake. These raids were driven by a combination of factors, including a desire for wealth, land, and a quest for adventure. The Viking raids were not mere acts of plunder; they were also precursors to more permanent settlements. The kingdom of Northumbria witnessed the establishment of a Viking stronghold at Jorvik, known today as York. Jorvik became a thriving trading center, reflecting the Norse aptitude for commerce and their integration into existing networks.

By the 9th century, the Viking presence had grown more significant. The Danelaw, a region in the north and east of England, was established through a series of agreements between the Anglo-Saxons and the Vikings. This marked a coexistence under a distinct set of laws and customs. The Danelaw was characterized by its urbanization, trade, and a blending of Anglo-Saxon and Norse cultures.

The Norse impact extended beyond political boundaries. Linguistically, Old Norse words became interwoven with Old English, enriching the language with new vocabulary. Place names, personal names, and even elements of law reflected this linguistic exchange, leaving an indelible mark on the evolution of the English language. The Danelaw also saw the integration of Norse deities and mythologies with existing beliefs. Temples and shrines dedicated to Norse gods were established alongside those of native deities. This syncretic approach exemplified the dynamic nature of cultural interactions during this time.

Despite the Viking reputation for raiding, it's important to note that not all Viking interactions were hostile. Settlements like the Isle of Man and the Hebrides served as trading hubs and centers of Norse influence. The Orkney and Shetland Islands, as well as parts of Scotland, were also under Norse control, leading to a fusion of Norse and Celtic cultures.

King Alfred the Great of Wessex played a significant role in stemming the Viking tide. His efforts to resist Viking incursions, along with the establishment of a network of fortified towns known as burhs, marked a turning point in the Anglo-Saxon struggle. The Treaty of Wedmore in 878 CE established a boundary between the Anglo-Saxon-controlled lands and the Danelaw.

The Viking Age in the British Isles eventually gave way to a process of assimilation and integration. The Scandinavian settlers and their descendants adopted local customs, intermarried with the native population, and embraced Christianity. The legacy of the Vikings can still be glimpsed in the names of towns, the genetic heritage of the population, and the tapestry of British culture.

Norman Conquest and Feudal England: A New Order Takes Root

The year 1066 stands as a pivotal moment in the history of the British Isles, forever altering the trajectory of the region. This was the year of the Norman Conquest, an event that ushered in a new era characterized by the establishment of a powerful feudal system and the infusion of Norman influences into the English cultural tapestry.

The stage for the Norman Conquest was set by the death of Edward the Confessor, the last Anglo-Saxon king of England, without a clear heir. This power vacuum led to a succession dispute between Harold Godwinson, an English nobleman, and William, Duke of Normandy. Claiming that Edward had promised him the English throne, William assembled an army and set his sights on conquering England.

In the famous Battle of Hastings in 1066, William's forces clashed with Harold's army. The battle ended with Harold's death and William's victory, solidifying his claim to the English crown. With this victory, William was crowned King of England and earned the moniker "William the Conqueror."

The Norman Conquest marked a profound turning point in the history of England. William's rule introduced a new aristocratic elite, with Norman nobles being granted extensive lands and titles in exchange for their loyalty and military service. The feudal system took root, establishing a hierarchical society where land was the primary source of wealth and power.

To consolidate his rule, William undertook a comprehensive survey of England's land and resources, known as the Domesday Book. Completed in 1086, this detailed record of property ownership and assets provided valuable insights into the social, economic, and administrative landscape of England at the time.

The Norman influence was not confined to politics and governance; it extended to culture, language, and architecture. The Normans brought their distinct Romanesque architectural style, characterized by rounded arches, thick walls, and ornate decorations. This style is exemplified by the construction of Durham Cathedral and the Tower of London, among others.

One of the most enduring legacies of the Norman Conquest is the transformation of the English language. The Normans spoke Old Norman, a language derived from Old Norse and Old French, and their interaction with the existing English population led to a blending of languages. The result was Middle English, a linguistic fusion that shaped the English language as we know it today.

William the Conqueror also sought to centralize his authority through the establishment of royal administrative institutions. The Exchequer, an early form of financial and administrative bureaucracy, was created to manage the kingdom's finances. This administrative structure laid the groundwork for a more organized and efficient governance system.

The Norman Conquest also had far-reaching consequences for England's relationship with continental Europe. The new monarchs maintained extensive land holdings in Normandy, leading to complex political entanglements and conflicts with other European powers. This continental connection continued to influence English politics and foreign affairs for centuries.

As the Norman Conquest unfolded, it left an indelible imprint on every facet of English society. The landscape was dotted with castles, abbeys, and cathedrals, each a testament to the architectural and cultural fusion of the era. The social hierarchy was redefined, and the English language evolved into a unique blend of linguistic traditions.

Plantagenets and the Hundred Years' War: Struggles for Supremacy

The Plantagenet dynasty emerged on the English throne in the 12th century, shaping the course of England's history for over three centuries. This period was marked by a tumultuous struggle for supremacy, epitomized by the Hundred Years' War—an epoch-defining conflict between England and France.

The Plantagenets came to power with Henry II, a dynamic ruler who expanded the realm's territories through strategic marriages and alliances. His marriage to Eleanor of Aquitaine brought substantial lands in France under English control. This Angevin Empire marked the zenith of Plantagenet influence, encompassing both sides of the English Channel.

The Plantagenet period saw remarkable legal developments. Henry II's establishment of a legal framework, known as the Common Law, laid the foundation for the modern English legal system. The introduction of juries and royal courts contributed to a more structured and efficient system of justice.

However, the Plantagenets faced internal conflicts as well. The rivalry between Henry II and his sons, particularly Richard the Lionheart and John Lackland, led to struggles over power and inheritance. John's reign saw the signing of the Magna Carta in 1215, a pivotal moment that curtailed the monarch's absolute authority and laid the groundwork for constitutional principles.

The 14th century marked the onset of the Hundred Years' War, a protracted conflict between England and France that endured for more than a century. The war had complex origins, including disputes over territorial claims, dynastic rivalries, and economic interests. The English monarchs' claims to the French crown ignited a series of conflicts that would profoundly impact both nations.

The early stages of the war saw notable successes for the English, particularly under Edward III and his son, the Black Prince. The Battle of Crécy in 1346 and the Battle of Poitiers in 1356 showcased English military prowess and the devastating impact of the English longbow on the battlefield.

The war's impact extended beyond military victories. The war accelerated the decline of feudalism and the rise of centralized power in both England and France. Financial strains from the war led to innovations such as the poll tax in England, further shaping the relationship between the monarchy and the populace.

One of the most iconic figures of the Hundred Years' War was Joan of Arc, a young French peasant girl who claimed to have received divine guidance to lead the French forces. Her efforts played a significant role in rallying French morale and turning the tide of the war in favor of France.

As the war progressed, England's territorial gains in France began to recede. The Treaty of Troyes in 1420, which recognized Henry V of England as heir to the French throne, failed to secure a lasting English hold over French territories. The conflict eventually culminated in the final expulsion of English forces from mainland France in the mid-15th century.

The Hundred Years' War left an indelible impact on both nations. It shaped military tactics, national identities, and the balance of power in Europe. The war's aftermath marked a period of introspection and reevaluation for England, leading to a period of political instability and dynastic upheavals.

War of the Roses: Yorkists and Lancastrians Clash for the Crown

The Wars of the Roses, a series of tumultuous conflicts that spanned several decades, stands as a pivotal chapter in English history. This period of strife and political upheaval was marked by a bitter struggle for the English crown between two rival factions: the Yorkists and the Lancastrians.

The origins of the Wars of the Roses can be traced back to the longstanding feud between the Houses of Lancaster and York. The conflict was rooted in complex familial and political dynamics, with both houses claiming legitimacy to the English throne. The Lancastrians traced their lineage to King Henry IV, while the Yorkists derived their claim through the line of Richard of York.

The feud ignited in earnest during the reign of King Henry VI, a Lancastrian monarch whose rule was marred by political instability and military defeats in France. Henry's mental instability further exacerbated the turmoil, leading to a power vacuum that both factions sought to exploit.

The Wars of the Roses commenced in 1455 with the First Battle of St Albans, where the Yorkists clashed with the Lancastrians in a violent confrontation. The Yorkists, led by Richard, Duke of York, emerged victorious in this initial battle, and Richard briefly assumed control of the government as Protector of the Realm.

However, the conflict was far from resolved. Henry VI's wife, Margaret of Anjou, remained a formidable figure in the Lancastrian camp. Her efforts to secure her son's claim to the throne added fuel to the fire, leading to further confrontations on the battlefield.

The Wars of the Roses were marked by a series of battles and skirmishes, including the Battles of Towton, Barnet, and Tewkesbury. These clashes resulted in shifting fortunes, with victories and defeats alternating between the two factions. The Battle of Towton in 1461, a decisive Yorkist triumph, saw Edward, Duke of York, crowned as Edward IV.

The intricate web of alliances and betrayals added complexity to the conflict. The intervention of foreign powers, including Burgundy and France, further fueled the chaos. The Wars of the Roses also witnessed the rise of influential figures like Richard Neville, Earl of Warwick, known as the "Kingmaker," whose allegiances played a pivotal role in determining the course of events.

The Yorkist reign under Edward IV brought a degree of stability, but it was not immune to internal strife. Edward's sudden death in 1483 led to a power struggle within the Yorkist camp. His young son, Edward V, was declared king, but his uncle, Richard, Duke of Gloucester (later Richard III), assumed the role of Protector.

Richard III's ascent to the throne marked a turning point in the Wars of the Roses. His controversial reign was marred by accusations of tyranny and political intrigue. The death of Edward IV's sons, famously known as the "Princes in the Tower," remains one of the enduring mysteries of this period.

The Wars of the Roses ultimately came to an end in 1487 with the Battle of Bosworth. Henry Tudor, a distant Lancastrian claimant with ties to the Welsh nobility, defeated Richard III and ascended the throne as Henry VII. This marked the beginning of the Tudor dynasty, which would bring a measure of stability and transformation to England.

Tudor Dynasty: The Era of Renaissance and Reformation

The Tudor dynasty, spanning from 1485 to 1603, occupies a distinctive place in English history. This era witnessed profound transformations in politics, culture, religion, and society, characterized by the Renaissance's intellectual revival and the Reformation's religious upheaval.

Henry VII, the founder of the Tudor dynasty, came to power after defeating Richard III at the Battle of Bosworth in 1485. His reign marked a departure from the tumultuous Wars of the Roses, as he sought to consolidate his rule and establish financial stability through prudent fiscal policies. The establishment of the Court of Star Chamber enhanced royal authority in legal matters, curbing the power of the nobility.

The era of the Tudors witnessed the blossoming of the Renaissance in England. The influence of Renaissance humanism, with its emphasis on learning, classical scholarship, and cultural refinement, permeated the courts and intellectual circles. Henry VII's court boasted scholars like Erasmus, who played a pivotal role in spreading Renaissance ideas.

Henry VIII, one of the most iconic Tudor monarchs, ushered in a period of significant change. His pursuit of a male heir led to the annulment of his marriage to Catherine of Aragon and his break from the Roman Catholic Church. The establishment of the Church of England under royal supremacy was a crucial step in the English Reformation.

The dissolution of the monasteries, beginning in the 1530s, marked a turning point in the religious and social landscape. Monastic properties were seized by the Crown, leading to the redistribution of land and wealth. This act not only shifted the economic balance but also paved the way for a more secularized society.

Henry VIII's reign was followed by the turbulent reign of his son, Edward VI. Edward's short rule witnessed a more pronounced Protestant agenda, as the Book of Common Prayer was introduced to standardize Anglican worship. Edward's reign also saw the rise of powerful Protestant reformers like Thomas Cranmer, Archbishop of Canterbury.

The pendulum swung once more with the accession of Mary I, known as "Bloody Mary" for her fervent efforts to restore Catholicism. Mary's short and tumultuous reign was marked by religious persecutions, aimed at reestablishing Catholic orthodoxy. The executions of Protestant leaders, including Thomas Cranmer, left a deep scar on the era.

The tide turned again with the ascent of Elizabeth I in 1558. Her reign marked a golden age for England, characterized by stability, expansion, and cultural flourishing. Elizabeth's shrewd diplomacy, exemplified by her handling of the Spanish Armada in 1588, secured England's position on the international stage.

Elizabethan England was a time of literary brilliance, with luminaries like William Shakespeare, Christopher Marlowe, and Edmund Spenser producing enduring works that have left an indelible mark on world literature. The English Renaissance saw the flourishing of drama, poetry, and the sonnet tradition, reflecting both intellectual and artistic vitality.

The Elizabethan era was not without its challenges, particularly the ongoing religious tensions. The Elizabethan Religious Settlement sought to strike a balance between Protestant and Catholic influences, resulting in the formation of the Church of England as a distinctive via media.

Elizabethan Glory: England's Golden Age on the World Stage

The Elizabethan era, named after the iconic Queen Elizabeth I, is often referred to as England's Golden Age. This period, spanning from the late 16th century into the early 17th century, witnessed a remarkable flourishing of culture, exploration, and political stability that elevated England to unprecedented heights on the global stage.

One of the defining features of the Elizabethan era was the expansion of England's influence beyond its shores. The era was marked by a wave of exploration, spurred on by the spirit of adventure and a desire for trade and conquest. The establishment of colonies and trading posts in far-flung corners of the world laid the foundation for England's future imperial ambitions.

The voyages of explorers like Sir Francis Drake and Sir Walter Raleigh captured the imaginations of the English people. Drake's circumnavigation of the globe in the late 16th century and his daring raids against Spanish treasure ships earned him a legendary status. Raleigh's efforts in establishing the Roanoke colony in the Americas highlighted England's growing interest in colonization.

England's naval power, embodied by the iconic warships of the era, such as the "Golden Hind," became a symbol of national pride. The defeat of the Spanish Armada in 1588, a naval battle that saw England emerge victorious against the mighty Spanish fleet, marked a pivotal moment in world history. The victory solidified England's status as a rising maritime power and secured its place in the annals of military achievement.

The Elizabethan era was not only marked by military prowess but also by a cultural renaissance. The works of playwrights like William Shakespeare, Christopher Marlowe, and Ben Jonson epitomized the era's literary brilliance. The Globe Theatre in London became a hub of artistic activity, presenting timeless plays that continue to captivate audiences to this day.

Shakespeare, often hailed as the greatest playwright in the English language, penned masterpieces like "Romeo and Juliet," "Hamlet," and "Macbeth." His ability to capture the complexities of the human experience and craft characters that resonate across time and cultures is a testament to the era's intellectual vibrancy.

The Elizabethan era also saw significant advancements in the fields of science and exploration. Sir Francis Bacon, often referred to as the father of empiricism, laid the groundwork for the scientific method and advocated for systematic observation and experimentation. Explorers like Sir Walter Raleigh contributed to the expansion of geographical knowledge through their voyages.

The era's architectural and artistic achievements are also noteworthy. The Elizabethan architectural style, characterized by ornate detailing and intricate timber framing, left a distinct mark on English buildings. Portraits and artworks from the era, including the "Ditchley Portrait" of Elizabeth I by Marcus Gheeraerts the Younger, offer insights into the fashions, aesthetics, and self-presentation of the time.

The Elizabethan era was also marked by a vibrant court culture. Queen Elizabeth's reign saw the emergence of a sophisticated and cultured court that attracted artists, poets, musicians, and scholars. Elizabeth herself was known for her strategic use of symbolism and imagery to project an aura of majesty and authority.

The Elizabethan era was not without its challenges, including religious tensions, economic disparities, and political intrigue. The Gunpowder Plot of 1605, an attempt to assassinate King James I and his government, underscored the ongoing religious divisions and conspiratorial undercurrents.

Stuart Turmoil: From Union to Civil War

The Stuart dynasty, which ruled England, Scotland, and later the entire British Isles, brought with it a period of significant upheaval and transformation. This chapter in history, stretching from the early 17th century to the mid-17th century, saw the union of England and Scotland, the execution of a monarch, and the eruption of a brutal civil war that would reshape the nation's destiny.

The Stuart era began with the accession of James VI of Scotland to the English throne as James I of England in 1603, marking the union of the two kingdoms under a single monarch. This union, known as the Union of the Crowns, paved the way for political and cultural interactions between England and Scotland.

James I, a proponent of the theory of divine right of kings, believed in the absolute authority of the monarch and clashed with Parliament over issues of taxation and governance. His attempts to assert royal authority led to tensions that would intensify during the reign of his son, Charles I.

Charles I's reign was marked by a struggle for power between the monarchy and Parliament. Financial difficulties and disputes over religious practices, particularly Charles's imposition of Anglican rituals on the Presbyterian Church of Scotland, ignited tensions. The king's attempts to levy taxes without parliamentary approval further fueled discontent.

The Petition of Right in 1628, which sought to limit the king's power and affirm the rights of subjects, highlighted the growing conflict between Charles and Parliament. Charles's dissolution of Parliament in 1629 marked a period of Personal Rule, during which he ruled without parliamentary consent, deepening mistrust and raising concerns over religious freedom.

Religious tensions added to the turmoil of the era. The spread of Puritanism and divergent religious beliefs led to a polarized society. Charles's efforts to impose religious uniformity, including the promotion of the Book of Common Prayer in Scotland, triggered the Bishops' Wars, conflicts between England and Scotland in the mid-17th century.

The culmination of tensions between Charles and Parliament came to a head in the English Civil War, also known as the War of the Three Kingdoms, which began in 1642. The conflict pitted the Royalists, loyal to Charles I, against the Parliamentarians, who sought greater influence in governance. The war saw brutal battles, sieges, and shifting allegiances, and it led to the temporary overthrow of the monarchy.

The war ended in 1649 with the execution of Charles I, an unprecedented event that sent shockwaves across Europe. The establishment of the Commonwealth, led by Oliver Cromwell, marked a radical departure from monarchy. Cromwell's rule, however, was characterized by religious restrictions, suppression of dissent, and the imposition of a more authoritarian regime.

The Stuart monarchy was restored in 1660 with the accession of Charles II, son of Charles I. The period following the Restoration saw efforts to reconcile the monarchy and Parliament, leading to the Glorious Revolution of 1688. This event resulted in the deposition of James II and the ascension of William III and Mary II to the throne, marking a pivotal moment in the evolution of constitutional monarchy in England.

The Commonwealth and Restoration: Shifting Powers and Perspectives

The period following the execution of Charles I and the establishment of the Commonwealth marked a dramatic shift in England's political landscape. The interregnum, led by Oliver Cromwell, and the subsequent Restoration of the monarchy under Charles II brought about profound changes in governance, religion, and society.

The Commonwealth, established in 1649 after the execution of Charles I, represented a radical departure from traditional monarchical rule. Oliver Cromwell, a skilled military leader and staunch Puritan, assumed the role of Lord Protector. The Commonwealth was characterized by religious fervor, republican ideals, and a determination to create a more just society.

Cromwell's rule was marked by a complex interplay of political, military, and religious factors. His Protectorate sought to maintain order while promoting Puritan values and suppressing perceived vices. The Rump Parliament, the legislative body during this period, reflected the tensions between more radical and more moderate elements within the Commonwealth.

Cromwell's foreign policy was dynamic, as he pursued an expansionist agenda and emerged as a powerful figure on the European stage. His campaigns in Ireland and Scotland aimed to consolidate his authority and bring these regions under English control. The brutality of his military campaigns, particularly in Ireland, remains a topic of historical debate and controversy.

The Commonwealth era also saw significant cultural shifts. Theatres were closed, and entertainment was tightly regulated to align with Puritan sensibilities. Educational reforms were introduced, and a new emphasis was placed on religious education and moral discipline.

The death of Oliver Cromwell in 1658 and the subsequent decline of the Protectorate led to a period of political uncertainty. His son, Richard Cromwell, briefly assumed power, but his rule was marked by internal divisions and a lack of strong leadership. This paved the way for the eventual Restoration of the monarchy.

The Restoration, marked by the return of Charles II to the throne in 1660, brought about a dramatic reversal of many Commonwealth-era policies. Theatres reopened, and the arts flourished once again. The king's own interests in science, culture, and philosophy influenced the court's atmosphere and cultivated an environment of intellectual inquiry.

The Restoration period also saw the reestablishment of the Church of England as the state church, bringing a measure of religious stability after the tumultuous years of religious experimentation. The Act of Uniformity in 1662 reaffirmed the Book of Common Prayer as the standard of worship, though it led to the ejection of nonconforming ministers from their pulpits.

The aftermath of the Restoration was marked by debates over religious freedom, political rights, and the role of Parliament. The emergence of political factions, notably the

Whigs and the Tories, highlighted differing visions for the nation's future governance.

Charles II's reign was followed by that of James II, whose Catholic faith raised concerns among Protestant elites. The Glorious Revolution of 1688, marked by the deposition of James II and the ascension of William III and Mary II, signaled a watershed moment in English history. The Declaration of Rights, a precursor to the Bill of Rights, established constitutional principles that curtailed the power of the monarch and affirmed the authority of Parliament.

Glorious Revolution: Constitutional Changes and the Rise of Parliament

The Glorious Revolution of 1688 stands as a pivotal moment in English history, heralding profound constitutional changes and reshaping the balance of power between the monarchy and Parliament. This bloodless revolution led to the ascension of William III and Mary II to the throne and laid the foundation for modern constitutional monarchy.

The events leading up to the Glorious Revolution were marked by increasing tensions between the monarchy and Parliament. King James II's Catholicism and his attempts to expand his authority fueled concerns among Protestant elites about the potential erosion of religious freedom and parliamentary rights.

In 1688, a group of English nobles and political figures invited William of Orange, a Dutch Protestant prince and Mary's husband, to intervene in English affairs. The invitation was extended partly due to fears that James II's newborn son might establish a Catholic dynasty, perpetuating religious and political tensions.

William's arrival in England marked a turning point. His forces faced minimal resistance, and James II fled to France, effectively abdicating the throne. In this power vacuum, William and Mary were offered the crown jointly, an event known as the "Declaration of Right" and later enshrined in the Bill of Rights of 1689.

The Bill of Rights set out a series of fundamental constitutional principles. It affirmed the rights of Parliament to make laws and levy taxes, prohibited the monarch from suspending laws or levying taxes without Parliament's consent, and asserted the rights of subjects to petition the king without fear of retribution. It also established the principle of regular parliamentary elections and laid the groundwork for a constitutional monarchy.

The Glorious Revolution was characterized by its bloodlessness. Unlike previous political upheavals, this transition of power occurred with relatively little violence or turmoil. It highlighted the growing consensus among the political elite that governance should be based on shared principles and the rule of law, rather than absolute monarchical authority.

The revolution had lasting implications for the balance of power between the monarchy and Parliament. The monarch's authority was curtailed, and the principle of parliamentary sovereignty gained prominence. The monarch's ability to govern without Parliament's consent was effectively limited, and the concept of a "constitutional monarchy" emerged.

The revolution also bolstered religious tolerance and freedom. The Toleration Act of 1689 granted limited religious freedom to dissenters, including non-Anglican Protestants, allowing them to worship openly and hold public office. However, Catholics continued to face legal and political restrictions, reflecting lingering religious prejudices.

The Glorious Revolution transformed the political landscape of England. It marked a transition from a period of political uncertainty and religious conflict to a more stable and inclusive form of governance. The constitutional changes paved the way for the growth of parliamentary authority, the protection of individual rights, and the emergence of a more representative political system.

The Glorious Revolution's legacy extended beyond England. It served as a model for other nations seeking to establish constitutional limits on monarchical power. The principles enshrined in the Bill of Rights influenced the framing of the United States Constitution and continue to shape discussions about the balance of power and the rights of citizens in modern democracies.

Hanoverian Rule and Georgian Enlightenment: A Time of Intellectual Growth

The Hanoverian era, spanning from the early 18th century to the early 19th century, brought a period of continuity and change to the British Isles. The Hanoverian monarchs, starting with George I, were of German origin and ushered in a time of political stability, economic expansion, and significant intellectual growth known as the Georgian Enlightenment.

George I's accession to the throne in 1714 marked the beginning of the Hanoverian dynasty's rule in Britain. The transition was not without challenges, as the Jacobite uprisings, aimed at restoring the Stuart monarchy, posed a threat to the new dynasty's legitimacy. The defeat of the Jacobite forces at the Battle of Culloden in 1746 solidified Hanoverian authority and marked the decline of Jacobitism as a significant political force.

The Georgian era witnessed profound changes in society, economics, and culture. The period saw the growth of urban centers, the expansion of trade and industry, and the emergence of a middle class with increased social and economic influence. The Agricultural Revolution led to innovations in farming techniques and contributed to a significant increase in agricultural productivity.

The Georgian Enlightenment, often considered an extension of the broader European Enlightenment, was characterized by a surge in intellectual curiosity, scientific inquiry, and cultural exchange. The rise of coffeehouses, salons, and learned societies provided spaces for individuals to engage in intellectual discussions and debates.

The flourishing of literature, art, and philosophy during the Georgian Enlightenment had a lasting impact on British culture. Writers like Jonathan Swift, Alexander Pope, and Samuel Johnson produced enduring literary works that continue to shape the English literary canon. Johnson's "A Dictionary of the English Language," published in 1755, was a monumental achievement that standardized the English language and reflected the era's commitment to intellectual rigor.

Scientific advancements were also a hallmark of the Georgian Enlightenment. The Royal Society, founded in the 17th century, continued to foster scientific inquiry, leading to discoveries in fields such as astronomy, medicine, and chemistry. Sir Isaac Newton's groundbreaking work in physics laid the foundation for modern scientific thought.

The period's architecture and urban planning also reflected Enlightenment ideals. The neoclassical architectural style, inspired by ancient Greece and Rome, became fashionable. Landmark structures like John Nash's Regent Street and the British Museum showcased the fusion of artistic expression and intellectual aspirations.

The Georgian era was not without its challenges. The growth of industrialization brought about urbanization and exacerbated social inequalities. The "Enclosure Movement," which consolidated land ownership and displaced rural communities, sparked tensions and unrest in certain regions.

The monarchy's role in governance evolved during the Georgian era. The monarchs began to play a more ceremonial and symbolic role, while political power gradually shifted towards Parliament. The establishment of the Prime Minister's office as the head of government marked a pivotal development in Britain's evolving political structure.

The Georgian era also saw the expansion of the British Empire, with the acquisition of new territories and the growth of overseas trade. The Seven Years' War, fought between 1756 and 1763, established Britain's global dominance and significantly expanded its colonial holdings.

Industrial Revolution: Transforming Society, Economy, and Landscapes

The Industrial Revolution, a period of profound technological, economic, and social change, had a transformative impact on Britain and the world. Spanning from the late 18th century to the mid-19th century, this era marked a shift from agrarian economies to industrialized societies, fundamentally altering the way people lived and worked.

The Industrial Revolution was characterized by a series of technological innovations that revolutionized various industries. The invention of the steam engine by James Watt in the 1760s was a pivotal breakthrough that powered factories, locomotives, and ships. This source of power laid the foundation for mechanization and the rise of factories.

The textile industry was at the forefront of industrialization. The spinning jenny, water frame, and power loom revolutionized textile production, enabling the mass production of fabrics. Factories emerged as centers of production, leading to urbanization as people migrated from rural areas to work in manufacturing hubs.

The coal and iron industries experienced significant growth during the Industrial Revolution. The expansion of coal mining provided a reliable source of energy for steam engines and other industrial processes. The use of iron in construction and machinery paved the way for the development of railways, bridges, and factories.

The transportation sector underwent a revolutionary transformation. The construction of canals and, later, the rapid expansion of railways improved the movement of goods and people across the country. Railways played a critical role in connecting industrial centers, fostering economic growth and urbanization.

Urbanization was a defining feature of the Industrial Revolution. The growth of factories and industries drew people to cities, leading to overcrowded and unsanitary living conditions in urban slums. This shift from rural to urban living reshaped social structures and led to the emergence of working-class communities.

The factory system revolutionized labor practices. Factory work introduced standardized working hours, division of labor, and increased efficiency. However, it also led to poor working conditions, including long hours, low wages, and limited safety regulations. Labor movements and trade unions emerged in response to these challenges.

The Industrial Revolution had a profound impact on society and culture. The rise of factories and urban living altered traditional social roles and family dynamics. Children and women became an integral part of the workforce, often working in harsh conditions. The Romantic movement emerged as a response to the mechanization of society, emphasizing emotion, nature, and individual expression in art and literature.

Economic growth was a hallmark of the Industrial Revolution. The expansion of industries and technological innovations led to increased production and trade. Capitalism flourished as entrepreneurs and investors sought to capitalize on new opportunities, leading to the accumulation of wealth and the rise of the bourgeoisie.

The Industrial Revolution also spurred advancements in science and technology. Innovations in machinery, chemistry, and engineering paved the way for further progress. The development of the telegraph and improvements in communication facilitated global connections and the exchange of ideas.

Environmental impacts were a consequence of industrialization. The reliance on coal and other resources led to pollution and deforestation. The growth of urban areas strained resources and contributed to poor sanitation and public health.

The Industrial Revolution's impact extended beyond Britain's borders. It influenced other nations to adopt similar industrialization processes, shaping global economic and social structures. It also laid the groundwork for future technological advancements and the continued evolution of societies.

British Empire Unveiled: Expansion, Colonies, and Global Dominance

The British Empire, spanning the 16th to the 20th centuries, was one of history's most extensive and influential colonial empires. Its expansion, marked by exploration, conquest, and colonization, played a pivotal role in shaping the modern world's political, economic, and cultural landscape.

The empire's foundations were laid during the Age of Exploration, with explorers like John Cabot and Francis Drake venturing to distant lands. The establishment of the East India Company in 1600 marked the beginning of British trade and influence in Asia. The colonization of Ireland, beginning in the 16th century, set the stage for imperial expansion.

The 18th century saw a significant acceleration of colonial acquisition. The acquisition of Canada after the Seven Years' War in 1763 further solidified British dominance in North America. The Thirteen Colonies, however, sought independence, leading to the American Revolutionary War and the birth of the United States in 1776.

The 19th century marked the zenith of British imperial expansion. The Industrial Revolution fueled demand for raw materials and markets, leading to the colonization of vast territories. Africa and Asia became targets for colonization, with British territories stretching from India to Australia.

India, known as the "Jewel in the Crown," was one of the most significant British colonies. The British East India Company's control eventually led to direct British rule in the Indian subcontinent. The impacts of British colonization on India's culture, economy, and society remain subjects of study and debate.

The colonization of Africa saw the establishment of territories such as South Africa, Nigeria, and Kenya. The "Scramble for Africa" saw European powers, including Britain, carving up the continent for resources and geopolitical advantage. This era brought both economic development and cultural challenges to African societies.

The British Empire's global dominance was facilitated by its naval power. The Royal Navy ensured the security of trade routes and facilitated communication between distant colonies. The empire's naval supremacy was showcased in landmark events like the Battle of Trafalgar in 1805.

The British Empire's impact extended beyond political control. It played a significant role in the spread of British culture, language, and legal systems. The English language became a lingua franca in many parts of the world, and British institutions influenced governance and education in colonies.

The empire also brought significant economic changes. The expansion of trade networks facilitated the exchange of goods and ideas across continents. The growth of the British merchant class and the emergence of a global market led to economic interconnectedness.

However, the empire was not without controversy and resistance. Colonial rule often led to exploitation, cultural suppression, and conflicts with indigenous populations. Movements for self-determination and independence emerged in various colonies, challenging British dominance.

World War I marked a turning point for the British Empire. The war's impact weakened the empire economically and militarily, and the rise of nationalist movements accelerated decolonization. World War II further strained imperial resources, leading to a post-war shift in global power dynamics.

The aftermath of World War II saw a wave of decolonization, as colonies sought independence from imperial rule. India gained independence in 1947, followed by many African and Asian nations. The process of decolonization reshaped the political map and global relationships.

The British Empire's legacy is complex. It left an enduring mark on the world's cultural, political, and economic landscape. While it brought advancements and connections, it also left a legacy of exploitation, inequality, and cultural imposition. The empire's rise, dominance, and eventual decline reflect the complexities of human history and the ever-evolving nature of global power dynamics.

Napoleonic Wars and Wellington's Triumph: A Nation at War

The Napoleonic Wars, a series of conflicts spanning from the late 18th to the early 19th century, reshaped the political and military landscape of Europe. The wars were marked by the ambitions of Napoleon Bonaparte, a charismatic military leader who rose to power in revolutionary France and sought to establish a European empire under his control.

The roots of the Napoleonic Wars can be traced back to the French Revolution. Napoleon, a brilliant military strategist, emerged as a prominent figure during the chaotic period of revolutionary upheaval. His rise to power culminated in the coup d'état of 1799, which established him as First Consul and later Emperor of the French in 1804.

Napoleon's ambitions extended far beyond France's borders. He sought to expand the French Empire through military conquest and diplomatic maneuvering. The wars that followed were characterized by rapid changes in territorial control, shifting alliances, and grand battles that reshaped the map of Europe.

The British Isles were not immune to the conflict. The Napoleonic Wars led to a series of confrontations between Britain and France, with the Royal Navy playing a pivotal role in securing British interests and maintaining control of maritime trade routes. The Battle of Trafalgar in 1805, where Admiral Lord Nelson led the British fleet to a decisive victory against the combined French and Spanish fleets, marked a turning point in naval warfare and solidified British naval supremacy.

The Peninsular War, fought on the Iberian Peninsula from 1808 to 1814, was a critical theater of the Napoleonic Wars. The Duke of Wellington, Arthur Wellesley, led British and Portuguese forces against the French, demonstrating his strategic brilliance in a series of successful campaigns. The Battle of Waterloo in 1815, where Wellington commanded British, Dutch, Belgian, and Prussian forces, culminated in Napoleon's defeat and marked the end of his reign.

The Napoleonic Wars had far-reaching effects on Britain's society and economy. The conflict required vast resources, leading to increased taxation and economic strain. The wars also brought social change, as military service became an avenue for social mobility, and the experience of war shaped the nation's collective identity.

The wars were not without controversy. The British government's use of press gangs to forcibly recruit sailors, the suppression of dissent, and economic disruptions raised concerns among the populace. The Luddite movement, a response to the mechanization of industries during the war, saw workers protesting against the loss of jobs and livelihoods.

Wellington's triumph at Waterloo was celebrated across Britain and Europe. The defeat of Napoleon marked a turning point in European history, leading to his exile to the island of Saint Helena. The Congress of Vienna in 1815 aimed to restore stability to Europe after the years of conflict, redrawing borders and establishing a balance of power among the major European nations.

The legacy of the Napoleonic Wars is enduring. The wars accelerated technological innovations, military tactics, and political alliances. They contributed to the rise of nationalism and the reshaping of European political systems. The wars also set the stage for Britain's emergence as a global superpower and the subsequent Pax Britannica, a period of relative peace and British dominance in the 19th century.

Victorian Splendor: Progress, Reform, and the Height of Empire

The Victorian era, spanning from 1837 to 1901, was a period of remarkable transformation and cultural refinement in the United Kingdom. Named after Queen Victoria, who ascended to the throne in 1837, this era was characterized by a unique blend of progress, social reform, and imperial expansion.

The Victorian era saw unprecedented economic growth driven by industrialization. The expansion of railways, the proliferation of factories, and advancements in technology fueled urbanization and contributed to a rising standard of living for some segments of society. The era marked a shift from an agrarian to an industrial economy, with coal, textiles, and steel industries driving economic progress.

This era also saw significant advancements in science and technology. The works of Charles Darwin, particularly "On the Origin of Species" published in 1859, revolutionized the understanding of evolution and the natural world. Innovations such as the telegraph and the steam engine continued to shape communication and transportation.

The Victorian era's cultural expressions were characterized by a fascination with progress and the exotic. The Great Exhibition of 1851, held in the Crystal Palace in London, showcased technological and artistic achievements from around the world. The exhibition's success highlighted Britain's global influence and marked a celebration of industry, innovation, and imperial achievement.

Social reform was a defining aspect of the Victorian era. Influenced by concerns about working conditions and social inequality, efforts were made to improve the lives of the working class. The Factory Acts of the mid-19th century aimed to regulate working hours and conditions, particularly for women and children. The Poor Law reforms aimed to provide assistance to the destitute while encouraging self-sufficiency.

Education reform also gained prominence during this era. The Elementary Education Act of 1870 aimed to provide elementary education to all children. The expansion of educational opportunities paved the way for increased social mobility and a more educated workforce.

The Victorian era witnessed a gradual expansion of political rights. The Reform Acts of 1832, 1867, and 1884 extended voting rights to a broader segment of the population. These reforms were a response to growing demands for representation and political participation.

The British Empire reached its zenith during the Victorian era. Colonial holdings expanded across Africa, Asia, and the Pacific, driven by economic interests, exploration, and strategic considerations. The era's imperial dominance was showcased in the phrase "the sun never sets on the British Empire," reflecting the vast expanse of territories under British control.

Cultural production flourished during this era. Literature, art, and architecture reflected the values and concerns of Victorian society. Novels by authors like Charles Dickens and Thomas Hardy explored the complexities of urban life, social inequality, and individual morality. Architecture embraced the neo-Gothic style, with landmarks like the

Palace of Westminster exemplifying the era's aesthetic sensibilities.

The Victorian era also brought challenges and contradictions. While progress and reform were being championed, issues like women's rights, labor rights, and sanitary conditions remained contentious. The "Woman Question" emerged as a topic of debate, sparking discussions about women's suffrage and gender roles.

The Victorian era came to an end with the death of Queen Victoria in 1901. Her reign, the longest in British history at the time, left an indelible mark on the nation and the world. The Victorian legacy is one of contrasts—of progress and inequality, imperial glory and social reform—a complex tapestry that continues to shape contemporary discussions about society, culture, and progress.

Highland Clearances and Irish Famine: Dark Clouds Over the Isles

The 18th and 19th centuries brought significant hardships to the British Isles, with the Highland Clearances in Scotland and the Irish Potato Famine casting dark shadows over the region. These events had profound social, economic, and cultural impacts that continue to shape the collective memory of the peoples of the Isles.

The Highland Clearances, spanning from the late 18th century to the mid-19th century, were a series of forced displacements of rural communities in the Scottish Highlands. Driven by economic pressures, landowners sought to replace traditional agriculture with more profitable sheep farming. This led to the eviction of tenant farmers and the destruction of traditional Highland society.

The Clearances had devastating consequences for the affected communities. Families were forced off their ancestral lands, often with little or no compensation, and left to seek new livelihoods in urban areas or across the Atlantic in North America. The upheaval shattered cultural bonds, leading to the loss of Gaelic language, traditions, and ways of life.

The Irish Potato Famine, also known as the Great Famine, occurred in the mid-19th century and had a profound impact on Ireland. The failure of the potato crop, a staple food for the Irish population, led to widespread starvation, disease, and death. The famine was exacerbated by British colonial policies, economic inequalities, and inadequate relief efforts.

The Great Famine resulted in the deaths of an estimated one million people and forced many others to emigrate in search of a better life. The population of Ireland, which had been heavily reliant on potatoes for sustenance, was decimated. The famine left a lasting scar on the nation's psyche and played a role in shaping Irish national identity and the struggle for independence.

The responses to these crises varied. While some landowners and officials justified the Clearances and their impact as necessary for economic progress, others condemned the forced displacements and cultural destruction. Similarly, the British government's handling of the Irish Famine remains a topic of historical debate, with criticisms of inadequate relief efforts and the continuation of exploitative colonial policies.

Both the Clearances and the Irish Famine contributed to waves of emigration. Scots and Irish alike sought new opportunities in the United States, Canada, and other parts of the British Empire. These migrations led to the dispersion of Highland and Irish cultures across the globe, resulting in diaspora communities that retained their cultural heritage.

The impact of these events on the British Isles reverberates in modern times. The memory of the Clearances and the Famine serves as a reminder of the complexities of power, economics, and social justice. The experiences of displacement, loss, and survival have influenced literature, music, and art, contributing to a deeper understanding of the historical trauma endured by these communities.

Efforts have been made to remember and honor the victims of these dark episodes. Memorials, museums, and cultural initiatives aim to preserve the memory of those who suffered during the Clearances and the Famine. These efforts acknowledge the resilience of affected communities and the importance of acknowledging painful histories.

The Highland Clearances and the Irish Famine stand as cautionary tales about the far-reaching consequences of economic policies, colonialism, and the interplay of power dynamics. The legacies of these events continue to shape conversations about social justice, cultural heritage, and the responsibility of governments and societies to address the needs of vulnerable populations.

Edwardian Era: The Precursor to Modernity

The Edwardian era, named after King Edward VII who reigned from 1901 to 1910, marked a transitional period between the Victorian era and the modern age. This era was characterized by a complex interplay of cultural shifts, social change, and technological advancements that laid the groundwork for the 20th century.

The Edwardian era witnessed the continuation of technological progress that had begun during the Victorian period. Innovations such as the telephone, electric lighting, and the automobile further transformed daily life and communication. These advancements heralded a new era of convenience and connectivity, setting the stage for the rapid technological developments of the 20th century.

The era also saw shifts in social norms and attitudes. The rise of the suffragette movement, advocating for women's right to vote, challenged traditional gender roles and paved the way for increased political participation by women. The discussion of women's suffrage and broader gender equality began to gain prominence in public discourse.

Art and culture underwent significant transformations during the Edwardian era. The Arts and Crafts movement, which had its roots in the late 19th century, continued to influence artistic expression, emphasizing craftsmanship and a return to handcrafted goods. Modernist influences began to emerge, challenging traditional artistic conventions and preparing the ground for the artistic experimentation of the 20th century.

The Edwardian era also witnessed a surge in interest in the natural world. Scientific exploration and discoveries, coupled with the expansion of educational opportunities, fostered a growing fascination with the mysteries of the universe. The period saw the publication of pivotal works in physics, such as Albert Einstein's theory of relativity.

The era's geopolitical landscape was shaped by global events. The decline of the Ottoman Empire and the Balkan Wars contributed to growing tensions in Europe that would eventually culminate in World War I. The assassination of Archduke Franz Ferdinand of Austria-Hungary in 1914 marked a pivotal moment that triggered the outbreak of the war, bringing an end to the Edwardian era and thrusting the world into a new era of conflict.

The Edwardian era also witnessed the expansion of leisure and entertainment. The rise of cinema, with the Lumière brothers' first public screening in 1895, introduced a new form of entertainment that captivated audiences worldwide. Theaters, music halls, and other forms of mass entertainment flourished, reflecting changing tastes and urban lifestyles.

Economic growth and industrial progress continued to shape society during the Edwardian era. Urbanization and improved transportation networks facilitated the movement of people and goods. The era also saw the rise of consumer culture, as mass-produced goods became more accessible to a wider range of individuals.

Despite these advancements, the era was not without its challenges. Class inequalities persisted, with social stratification influencing access to education, healthcare, and economic opportunities. Labor disputes and the growing influence of socialist ideologies highlighted the tensions between labor and capital.

The Edwardian era's influence extended beyond its immediate time frame. The cultural shifts, technological advancements, and social movements laid the groundwork for the changes that would define the 20th century. As the world transitioned from horse-drawn carriages to automobiles, from gas lamps to electric lights, and from Victorian sensibilities to modernist experimentation, the Edwardian era set the stage for the seismic shifts that would follow.

World War I: Sacrifice and Societal Shifts

World War I, often referred to as the Great War, was a global conflict that erupted in 1914 and lasted until 1918. The war marked a watershed moment in world history, reshaping political, social, and economic landscapes, while exacting a heavy toll on human lives and societies across the globe.

The origins of World War I can be traced to a complex web of political alliances, imperial rivalries, and territorial disputes among European powers. The assassination of Archduke Franz Ferdinand of Austria-Hungary in 1914 by a Serbian nationalist sparked a chain reaction of events that led to declarations of war and the mobilization of forces.

The war quickly escalated, with military technology and tactics evolving to unprecedented levels. Trench warfare became a defining feature on the Western Front, characterized by deadly stalemates and brutal conditions. The use of new weapons, such as machine guns, tanks, and poison gas, contributed to the unprecedented scale of casualties.

World War I had far-reaching impacts on societies around the world. The war required the mobilization of entire populations, leading to a massive upheaval of daily life. Men were drafted into military service, leaving behind families, jobs, and communities. Women stepped into roles traditionally held by men, working in factories, farms, and other essential industries.

The war's impact on the home front was profound. Rationing and shortages of goods became common as resources were redirected to the war effort. Propaganda campaigns aimed to rally support for the war and promote national unity. Governments also imposed censorship and restrictions on civil liberties in the name of security.

The human cost of World War I was staggering. Millions of soldiers and civilians lost their lives, and many more were injured physically and mentally. The war's unprecedented scale of destruction left scars on landscapes and communities. The Battle of the Somme, fought in 1916, stands as a tragic symbol of the war's brutality, resulting in massive casualties for both sides.

The war also had a profound impact on cultural and artistic expression. The disillusionment and trauma experienced by soldiers gave rise to works of literature, poetry, and art that conveyed the horrors of war and the human struggle for meaning amidst chaos. Poets like Wilfred Owen and Siegfried Sassoon depicted the grim realities of combat, while artists like Otto Dix captured the war's psychological toll.

The war led to significant political changes. The fall of empires, such as the Austro-Hungarian and Ottoman Empires, reshaped the map of Europe and the Middle East. The Russian Revolution of 1917, triggered by economic hardships and discontent, led to the establishment of a communist government under the leadership of the Bolsheviks.

The Treaty of Versailles, signed in 1919, officially ended the war and imposed harsh terms on Germany. The treaty's punitive measures, including territorial losses, reparations, and military restrictions, sowed the seeds of future conflicts and contributed to Germany's economic and political instability.

World War I's legacy continues to be felt today. The war marked a turning point in international relations, leading to the establishment of the League of Nations, a precursor to the United Nations, in an effort to prevent future conflicts. The war's impact on technology, medicine, and communication laid the groundwork for advancements that shaped the 20th century.

The sacrifices made during World War I, along with the societal shifts it prompted, remain a reminder of the complexities of human conflict. The war's aftermath and the search for meaning amidst its devastation continue to influence discussions about peace, diplomacy, and the enduring quest for a more just and secure world.

Interwar Years: Between Two World Wars

The interwar years, spanning the period between the end of World War I in 1918 and the beginning of World War II in 1939, were a time of uncertainty, transformation, and upheaval. This era of relative calm between two global conflicts was marked by complex political dynamics, economic challenges, and societal shifts that laid the groundwork for the tumultuous events of the 20th century.

The aftermath of World War I set the stage for many of the developments of the interwar years. The Treaty of Versailles, which imposed punitive measures on Germany, contributed to economic instability and political resentment. The war's psychological trauma, coupled with disillusionment over the war's outcomes, left scars on societies across Europe.

Economic challenges played a central role during the interwar years. The Great Depression, which began in 1929 with the stock market crash in the United States, had a global impact, leading to mass unemployment, poverty, and social unrest. The economic hardships exacerbated existing tensions and created fertile ground for extremist ideologies to take root.

Political ideologies and movements gained prominence during the interwar years. Fascism, characterized by authoritarianism, nationalism, and militarism, gained traction in countries like Italy under Benito Mussolini and Germany under Adolf Hitler. The rise of communism, inspired by the Russian Revolution, also saw the establishment of Soviet states and the spread of Marxist ideology.

The League of Nations, established after World War I with the aim of preventing future conflicts, faced challenges in maintaining global peace. The absence of major powers like the United States from the League's ranks weakened its effectiveness. Conflicts such as the Spanish Civil War and the Japanese invasion of Manchuria highlighted the limitations of international cooperation.

Artistic and cultural expressions underwent significant changes during the interwar years. The aftermath of World War I inspired movements like Dadaism and Surrealism, which challenged traditional artistic conventions and explored the complexities of the human experience. Literature, film, and art provided a means of processing the trauma of war and the anxieties of an uncertain future.

Social changes were also evident during this period. Women's suffrage movements gained momentum, leading to increased political participation and advocacy for gender equality. The war had disrupted traditional gender roles, and women's contributions during the conflict and the interwar period played a role in advancing women's rights.

Technological advancements continued to shape society during the interwar years. The spread of radio broadcasts, for instance, revolutionized communication and entertainment, reaching audiences beyond national borders. The aviation industry made significant strides, with Charles Lindbergh's solo transatlantic flight capturing the world's imagination.

Geopolitical tensions simmered beneath the surface during the interwar years. The rise of expansionist regimes and the rearmament of countries like Germany and Japan foreshadowed the conflicts that would follow. The appeasement policy, pursued by Western powers in the face of aggressive actions by Nazi Germany, highlighted the challenges of diplomacy in the face of rising militarism.

The interwar years came to an end with the outbreak of World War II in 1939, a conflict that would prove even more devastating than its predecessor. The lessons and legacies of the interwar period continue to be studied and debated, serving as a reminder of the complex interplay of political, economic, and societal factors that contribute to the shaping of history.

World War II: The United Kingdom's Defiant Stand

World War II, spanning from 1939 to 1945, was a global conflict that reshaped the course of history. For the United Kingdom, the war was marked by a resolute stand against aggression, a relentless spirit of resistance, and the unwavering determination of its people to defend their nation and ideals.

The war's origins can be traced to the aggressive expansionist policies of Nazi Germany under Adolf Hitler. The German invasion of Poland in September 1939 triggered the outbreak of hostilities, as Britain and France declared war in defense of Poland's sovereignty. The conflict soon escalated into a global struggle involving major powers from around the world.

The United Kingdom's response to the war was characterized by a steadfast commitment to opposing tyranny and upholding democratic values. Under the leadership of Prime Minister Winston Churchill, who assumed office in 1940, the British people rallied around the slogan "Keep Calm and Carry On," embodying the nation's resilience in the face of adversity.

The early years of the war were marked by a series of German military successes, including the fall of France in 1940. The British Expeditionary Force was evacuated from the beaches of Dunkirk in a daring rescue operation that saved the lives of hundreds of thousands of soldiers. The Battle of Britain, fought in the skies over the UK, saw the

Royal Air Force repel German air attacks, preventing a German invasion.

The Blitz, a sustained bombing campaign by the German Luftwaffe against British cities, inflicted heavy damage and casualties. London and other major cities were targeted, testing the resilience of the British people and their capacity to endure hardship. Despite the destruction, the spirit of unity and defiance remained unbroken.

The Battle of the Atlantic, a protracted naval struggle to protect vital supply lines, played a critical role in the war effort. The Royal Navy, along with allied forces, engaged in constant battles with German U-boats to ensure the safe passage of goods and troops. The development of convoy systems and technological advancements were crucial in turning the tide of the battle in favor of the Allies.

The United Kingdom's alliance with the United States and the Soviet Union, forming the "Big Three," marked a turning point in the war. The entry of the United States into the conflict after the attack on Pearl Harbor in 1941 brought immense industrial and military support to the Allies. The coordinated efforts of the Big Three culminated in a combined assault on Nazi-occupied Europe on D-Day in 1944.

The war effort required sacrifices from every sector of British society. Rationing and shortages were prevalent as resources were directed towards the military. Women played an essential role in the war effort, joining the workforce and serving in various capacities. The Home Guard, composed of civilian volunteers, provided defense on the home front.

The war ended in 1945 with the unconditional surrender of Germany. The United Kingdom's determination and sacrifice were instrumental in the defeat of Nazi tyranny. The war's impact on Britain was profound, leading to post-war reconstruction efforts, the establishment of the welfare state, and changes in colonial policies.

World War II's legacy in the United Kingdom is one of courage, unity, and the unwavering commitment to freedom. The nation's resilience and the sacrifices made during the conflict continue to be commemorated and honored. The war's lessons in the value of international cooperation and the horrors of totalitarianism remain relevant in shaping the world's understanding of conflict, peace, and the enduring pursuit of liberty.

Post-War Reconstruction: Rebuilding Amidst Challenges

The aftermath of World War II brought with it a complex landscape of destruction, displacement, and opportunity. The need to rebuild nations, economies, and societies after the devastating conflict posed unprecedented challenges and opportunities for the world, including the United Kingdom.

In the United Kingdom, post-war reconstruction was a monumental task that encompassed physical, economic, and social aspects. The war had left significant portions of the country in ruins, with cities like London bearing the scars of relentless bombing campaigns. Rebuilding required a combination of government planning, international assistance, and the resilience of the British people.

The immediate post-war years were characterized by shortages, rationing, and economic challenges. The war effort had strained resources and disrupted supply chains, leaving the country in a state of scarcity. Rationing continued for years after the war, affecting everything from food to clothing and fuel.

The government's commitment to rebuilding was evident in the establishment of programs aimed at revitalizing infrastructure and housing. The New Towns Act of 1946 sought to address housing shortages by creating new planned communities. The Beveridge Report of 1942 laid the foundation for the welfare state, advocating for social reforms and safety nets to support the population.

The economic challenges of post-war reconstruction were immense. The war had left the country deeply indebted, requiring careful management of finances and resources. Efforts to stimulate economic growth included investments in industries such as manufacturing and the expansion of public services.

International cooperation played a significant role in the post-war reconstruction effort. The Marshall Plan, launched by the United States in 1948, provided financial aid and resources to European nations, including the United Kingdom, to aid in their recovery. This support helped jumpstart economic recovery and stabilize the region.

The reintegration of veterans and displaced persons into society posed unique challenges. The demobilization of troops required careful planning to ensure a smooth transition to civilian life. The resettlement of refugees and displaced individuals, including those who had been evacuated during the war, required coordinated efforts to provide housing, employment, and support.

Cultural and artistic expressions also evolved in the post-war period. The war's impact on literature, film, and art led to the exploration of themes of trauma, memory, and the human experience. The rise of the "Angry Young Men" movement in literature reflected changing attitudes toward authority, social norms, and political institutions.

The decline of the British Empire marked a significant shift in the geopolitical landscape. The cost of the war and changing global dynamics led to decolonization efforts, granting independence to various colonies. The dismantling of the empire had far-reaching consequences for the United Kingdom's global influence and identity.

Post-war reconstruction was not without its challenges and criticisms. Social inequalities persisted, and efforts to address them often faced resistance. The dismantling of the wartime coalition government led to political realignments and the emergence of the Labour Party as a major political force.

The post-war period was also marked by the onset of the Cold War, a geopolitical rivalry between the United States and the Soviet Union. The United Kingdom found itself caught in the midst of this ideological struggle, navigating alliances and tensions on the international stage.

Post-war reconstruction efforts laid the foundation for the modern United Kingdom. The nation's ability to rebuild, adapt, and innovate demonstrated its resilience and determination in the face of adversity. The legacies of post-war reconstruction continue to influence discussions about social welfare, economic planning, and the enduring pursuit of stability and progress.

Welfare State and National Health Service: A New Social Landscape

The establishment of the welfare state and the introduction of the National Health Service (NHS) in the United Kingdom marked a transformative moment in the nation's history. These developments, born out of post-war reconstruction efforts, reshaped the social, economic, and healthcare landscapes, leaving an indelible impact on British society.

The idea of a welfare state emerged as a response to the social and economic challenges that followed World War II. The Beveridge Report of 1942, authored by economist William Beveridge, laid the groundwork for the welfare state by proposing a system of social insurance and assistance to provide a safety net for citizens. The report identified five "giant evils": want, disease, ignorance, squalor, and idleness, and called for comprehensive measures to address them.

The Labour Party, led by Prime Minister Clement Attlee, embraced the recommendations of the Beveridge Report and embarked on a program of radical social reform. The National Insurance Act of 1946 introduced measures to provide financial support for those unable to work due to sickness, unemployment, or old age. The National Assistance Act of the same year established a means-tested system of assistance for those in need.

The centerpiece of the post-war social reforms was the creation of the National Health Service in 1948. The NHS aimed to provide free and comprehensive healthcare services to all citizens, regardless of their financial means. The system was designed to ensure that access to medical care was based on need rather than ability to pay.

The establishment of the NHS was met with widespread support and enthusiasm. Prior to its introduction, healthcare services were often fragmented, with varying levels of access and quality. The NHS standardized medical care, making it available to everyone, and played a critical role in improving public health outcomes.

The NHS's inception marked a monumental shift in healthcare provision. It centralized medical services under a single system and removed financial barriers to healthcare access. Hospitals, clinics, and general practitioner services were integrated, streamlining patient care and medical administration.

The NHS's impact on public health was profound. It facilitated preventive care, health education, and vaccination programs, leading to a reduction in mortality rates for many diseases. Maternal and infant mortality rates also declined significantly, reflecting improved healthcare during pregnancy and childbirth.

The welfare state and the NHS contributed to the alleviation of poverty and social inequality. The introduction of social safety nets and healthcare services provided a safety net for vulnerable individuals and families, helping to lift them out of destitution and improving their overall well-being.

However, the implementation of the welfare state and the NHS was not without challenges. The cost of funding these initiatives and managing their operations required significant financial investments. The balance between expanding services and maintaining fiscal sustainability remained an ongoing concern.

The legacy of the welfare state and the NHS endures to this day. The principle of healthcare as a fundamental human right and the idea of social safety nets have become integral to British society's values and identity. Despite debates about funding and the role of the state in providing services, the commitment to ensuring access to healthcare and social support remains a cornerstone of the nation's ethos.

The establishment of the welfare state and the NHS transformed the United Kingdom's social landscape. These initiatives represented a departure from the laissez-faire policies of the past and reflected a new vision of the state's role in safeguarding the well-being of its citizens. The legacy of these reforms continues to shape discussions about social policy, equality, and the responsibilities of government in providing for the needs of its people.

Decolonization and End of Empire: The UK's Changing Global Role

The period of decolonization, spanning from the mid-20th century to the 1970s, marked a profound shift in the United Kingdom's global role and identity. This era saw the dismantling of the British Empire, as former colonies gained independence, and the United Kingdom navigated its changing position on the world stage.

The aftermath of World War II accelerated the decolonization process. The war had strained resources and exposed the vulnerabilities of imperial powers. Colonies had contributed to the war effort, and the war's ideological rhetoric of freedom and self-determination resonated with colonized populations.

India, the "Jewel in the Crown" of the British Empire, became a focal point of decolonization efforts. The Indian National Congress, led by figures like Mahatma Gandhi, advocated for independence and civil rights. The intense struggle for Indian independence culminated in the Indian Independence Act of 1947, which partitioned India into two nations: India and Pakistan.

Decolonization spread to other regions, as well. African nations, long subjected to colonial rule, began demanding self-governance and independence. The Gold Coast (now Ghana) gained independence in 1957, becoming the first sub-Saharan African nation to do so. Other nations in Africa followed suit, as the wave of decolonization swept across the continent.

The process of decolonization was complex and multifaceted. It involved negotiations, constitutional reforms, and in some cases, armed struggles. While some colonies achieved independence through peaceful means, others faced violent conflicts as they sought to break free from colonial rule.

The Suez Crisis of 1956 highlighted the challenges the United Kingdom faced as it relinquished control over its colonies. The crisis, triggered by the nationalization of the Suez Canal by Egyptian President Gamal Abdel Nasser, exposed the UK's waning influence and the limitations of its military power. The crisis also marked a turning point in relations between former colonial powers and their former colonies.

The decolonization process forced the United Kingdom to redefine its global role. As colonies gained independence, the British Empire gave way to the emergence of the Commonwealth of Nations. The Commonwealth represented a new form of association between former colonies and the UK, based on shared values, cooperation, and mutual respect.

The end of empire had significant implications for the United Kingdom's economy. The loss of colonial markets and resources necessitated a shift in economic priorities. The UK turned towards strengthening its ties with Europe and other global partners, diversifying its trade relationships, and exploring new economic opportunities.

Decolonization also had social and cultural impacts. It forced the British people to grapple with questions of national identity, multiculturalism, and their relationship with former colonies. The Windrush generation, migrants from Caribbean countries invited to the UK to help rebuild the nation after World War II, played a pivotal role in shaping discussions about immigration and diversity.

The legacy of decolonization continues to shape the United Kingdom's relationship with its former colonies and the global community. The Commonwealth remains an important forum for diplomatic, cultural, and economic cooperation. The process of reckoning with the legacies of empire, including issues of reparations and historical injustices, continues to be a topic of discussion and debate.

The era of decolonization marked a turning point in the United Kingdom's history, as the nation confronted the complexities of relinquishing imperial power and redefining its global identity. The process laid the groundwork for the UK's modern engagement with the world and its ongoing efforts to navigate its changing role in a rapidly evolving international landscape.

Cultural Revolution: Music, Arts, and Shifting Norms

The mid-20th century witnessed a cultural revolution in the United Kingdom that transformed artistic expression, challenged societal norms, and left an enduring impact on the nation's identity. This era of innovation and change was marked by shifts in music, art, literature, and social attitudes that reflected the evolving values of British society.

The post-war period saw the rise of various cultural movements that pushed the boundaries of traditional artistic conventions. In music, the emergence of rock and roll in the 1950s, influenced by American artists like Elvis Presley and Chuck Berry, revolutionized the musical landscape. British artists, such as The Beatles, The Rolling Stones, and The Who, took the world by storm with their distinctive sounds and rebellious attitudes.

The Swinging Sixties, a period of cultural upheaval and experimentation during the 1960s, brought about further transformation. London, particularly the neighborhood of Soho, became a hub of artistic activity. The fashion scene flourished, with figures like Mary Quant pioneering mod style, characterized by bold patterns, mini-skirts, and youthful exuberance.

The Beatles, with their innovative music and countercultural ethos, captured the spirit of the era. Their influence extended beyond music, shaping fashion, hairstyles, and attitudes towards individuality and creativity. The band's journey from Liverpool's Cavern Club to international stardom symbolized the changing landscape of British culture.

Literature also played a significant role in the cultural revolution. The Beat Generation, a group of writers and poets known for their rejection of societal norms, had a profound impact on British literature. Authors like Allen Ginsberg and Jack Kerouac inspired a new generation of British writers to explore themes of individualism, nonconformity, and social critique.

The Angry Young Men movement emerged as a response to the post-war establishment, challenging traditional class structures and questioning authority. Playwrights like John Osborne and literature figures like Kingsley Amis expressed disillusionment with post-war society, giving voice to the frustrations and aspirations of their generation.

Art underwent a transformation during this period, as well. The Pop Art movement, characterized by its use of popular culture imagery and vibrant colors, reflected the consumerism and mass media saturation of the era. Artists like Richard Hamilton and Peter Blake captured the essence of the Swinging Sixties in their works.

The cultural revolution also prompted shifts in social norms and attitudes. The advent of the birth control pill in the 1960s contributed to changing views on sexuality and reproductive rights. The legalization of homosexuality in 1967 marked a significant step towards greater acceptance and inclusion of LGBTQ+ individuals.

The feminist movement gained momentum during this period, advocating for women's rights, equality, and autonomy. Figures like Betty Friedan and Germaine Greer challenged gender roles and inspired a broader discussion about women's roles in society. The introduction of the Equal Pay Act in 1970 was a notable outcome of these efforts.

However, the cultural revolution was not without its challenges and criticisms. The increasing commercialization of music and art led to debates about authenticity and artistic integrity. Critics argued that the focus on consumerism and popular appeal diluted the subversive potential of cultural movements.

The legacy of the cultural revolution continues to shape British culture and society. The influence of the 1960s and its emphasis on individual expression, creative experimentation, and social change can still be seen in contemporary art, music, fashion, and social activism. The era's impact on attitudes towards gender, sexuality, and identity also resonates in ongoing discussions about equality and inclusion.

The cultural revolution of the mid-20th century remains a testament to the power of artistic expression to challenge norms, inspire change, and shape the course of history. The innovative spirit of this era continues to inspire new generations of artists, writers, musicians, and thinkers to push boundaries, question conventions, and contribute to the ongoing evolution of British culture.

Thatcher Era: Conservative Resurgence and Controversies

The Thatcher Era, spanning from 1979 to 1990, was a transformative period in the history of the United Kingdom. The leadership of Prime Minister Margaret Thatcher marked a resurgence of conservative ideology, economic reforms, and profound social changes that left an indelible impact on the nation.

Margaret Thatcher's premiership was characterized by a commitment to free-market capitalism, limited government intervention, and individualism. Known as "Thatcherism," her policies aimed to revitalize the British economy and reshape the social fabric of the country. One of her first acts was to implement monetarist policies to curb inflation, leading to a period of economic restructuring.

Thatcher's economic reforms, often referred to as "The Big Bang," deregulated financial markets and led to a surge in financial services in London. Privatization of state-owned industries was a central tenet of Thatcher's economic agenda. Utilities like British Telecom, British Gas, and British Airways were privatized, transforming them into privately-owned entities.

The confrontations between Thatcher's government and labor unions became a defining feature of her tenure. The early 1980s witnessed high-profile clashes, including the miners' strike of 1984-1985, which pitted the National Union of Mineworkers against the government's push for coal industry reforms. The strike was marked by violence, protests, and bitter divisions.

Thatcher's foreign policy was marked by assertiveness and strong alignment with the United States. The Falklands War of 1982, fought between the UK and Argentina over the Falkland Islands, showcased her resolute leadership style. The successful military operation to retake the islands bolstered her popularity and cemented her image as a strong and decisive leader.

Thatcher's social policies also left a significant impact on British society. Her emphasis on individualism and self-reliance sometimes led to criticisms that her policies disproportionately affected vulnerable populations. The introduction of the Poll Tax, a flat-rate tax on all adult residents, sparked widespread protests and opposition.

Controversies surrounding Thatcher's policies were not limited to domestic matters. Her stance on Europe, characterized by skepticism of deeper European integration, led to tense negotiations with European counterparts. She famously declared, "I want my money back," referring to her push for a fairer distribution of the UK's financial contributions to the European Economic Community.

Thatcher's tenure was marked by a deep ideological divide within the Conservative Party itself. The divide over Europe and her leadership style led to internal challenges. In 1990, amid mounting opposition, she was forced to resign as Prime Minister, marking the end of the Thatcher Era.

The legacy of the Thatcher Era remains complex and divisive. Supporters credit her with revitalizing the economy, reducing the power of trade unions, and championing individual liberty. Critics argue that her policies exacerbated social inequality, weakened the welfare state, and created divisions within society.

Thatcher's impact on British politics and society cannot be understated. Her leadership style, policies, and rhetoric continue to influence political debates and discussions about the role of government, economic priorities, and the balance between individual freedom and social responsibility. The Thatcher Era is a reminder of the power of political leadership to shape a nation's trajectory and provoke lasting debates about its direction.

New Millennium Challenges: Facing the 21st Century

The dawn of the 21st century ushered in a new era for the United Kingdom, marked by unprecedented challenges, technological advancements, and evolving global dynamics. As the nation navigated the complexities of a rapidly changing world, it confronted a range of issues that shaped its path in the new millennium.

The early years of the 21st century saw the United Kingdom adapting to a digital age characterized by rapid technological advancements. The proliferation of the internet, mobile devices, and social media transformed communication, commerce, and social interactions. The digital revolution posed both opportunities and challenges, from fostering innovation to grappling with concerns about privacy and cybersecurity.

Globalization became an increasingly defining feature of the 21st-century landscape. The interconnectedness of economies, cultures, and societies highlighted the importance of international cooperation and diplomacy. The United Kingdom's role in the European Union (EU) shaped its engagement with the global community, but discussions about its relationship with the EU intensified over the years.

The September 11, 2001 terrorist attacks in the United States had far-reaching consequences for global security and counterterrorism efforts. The UK, as a close ally of the US, joined international efforts to combat terrorism and participated in military interventions in Afghanistan and Iraq. These actions ignited debates about foreign policy, national security, and the ethical implications of military interventions.

The global financial crisis of 2008 had profound economic ramifications for the United Kingdom. The crisis exposed vulnerabilities in the financial sector and triggered a recession that impacted employment, housing, and public services. The government responded with stimulus packages and financial sector reforms aimed at stabilizing the economy.

Climate change emerged as a critical challenge in the 21st century, prompting discussions about sustainable development and environmental stewardship. The UK committed to reducing greenhouse gas emissions, transitioning to renewable energy sources, and playing a leading role in international climate negotiations.

Demographic shifts and immigration also played a significant role in shaping the United Kingdom's trajectory. Immigration patterns, including the arrival of skilled workers, refugees, and EU citizens, prompted debates about national identity, cultural integration, and the benefits of diversity.

The Brexit referendum of 2016 marked a pivotal moment in the UK's recent history. The decision to leave the European Union reflected divisions within the nation and ignited complex negotiations that reshaped the UK's relationship with its European neighbors. The process led to discussions about trade agreements, border controls, and the implications for various sectors of the economy.

Social and cultural issues took center stage in the 21st century as well. Debates about LGBTQ+ rights, gender equality, and racial justice gained prominence. Changes in societal attitudes towards marriage equality, gender identity, and representation reflected the evolving values of British society.

Technological advancements continued to drive change in various sectors, from healthcare to transportation. The advent of artificial intelligence, automation, and machine learning posed both opportunities and concerns about the future of work, education, and ethics.

The ongoing challenges of the 21st century underscored the need for adaptable and forward-thinking policies. The UK's response to crises such as the COVID-19 pandemic demonstrated its ability to mobilize resources, enact public health measures, and adapt to unprecedented circumstances.

As the United Kingdom navigates the challenges of the new millennium, it faces a complex web of issues that demand visionary leadership, international cooperation, and inclusive governance. The ability to address these challenges while preserving core values and fostering innovation will shape the nation's role in the global arena and influence the course of its history in the years to come.

Devolution and Rise of Scottish Nationalism: The Changing Political Map

The late 20th and early 21st centuries witnessed a significant transformation in the political landscape of the United Kingdom, driven by the devolution of powers to Scotland, Wales, and Northern Ireland. This era also saw the rise of Scottish nationalism, challenging the traditional notions of British identity and governance.

The movement for devolution gained momentum in the latter part of the 20th century as a response to demands for greater regional autonomy. In 1997, the Labour government, led by Prime Minister Tony Blair, introduced referendums in Scotland and Wales to determine whether they should have their own legislative bodies. Both referendums resulted in a majority vote in favor of devolution.

The Scotland Act of 1998 established the Scottish Parliament in Edinburgh, granting it powers over areas such as health, education, and transportation. The Wales Act of the same year created the National Assembly for Wales, giving it authority over issues including education and local government. Devolution marked a departure from the centuries-old tradition of centralized governance from London.

Devolution aimed to address the varying needs and aspirations of the different nations within the UK while maintaining a degree of unity. However, the process was not without challenges. The distribution of powers and the complexities of governance arrangements led to debates about the division of responsibilities and funding between the devolved administrations and the UK government.

The rise of Scottish nationalism, embodied by the Scottish National Party (SNP), became a significant force in the political landscape. The SNP's goal was to achieve Scottish independence and establish Scotland as an independent nation within the European Union. The party's success in elections to the Scottish Parliament and the UK Parliament brought the issue of independence to the forefront of public discourse.

The referendum on Scottish independence in 2014 marked a pivotal moment in the movement. The referendum saw intense campaigning and passionate debates on issues ranging from currency to EU membership. Ultimately, the "No" campaign prevailed, with 55.3% of voters choosing to remain part of the United Kingdom. However, the referendum had lasting effects, energizing the independence movement and reshaping political dynamics.

The Brexit referendum in 2016 further complicated the landscape. While the UK as a whole voted to leave the EU, Scotland voted overwhelmingly to remain. The disparity in voting patterns reignited discussions about Scottish independence, as many Scots felt that the Brexit decision did not reflect their preferences.

The political climate surrounding devolution and Scottish nationalism was complex and at times polarized. The UK government under Prime Minister David Cameron agreed to a new Scotland Act in 2016, granting additional powers to the Scottish Parliament. However, the question of independence remained a point of contention.

The Scottish Parliament's response to the COVID-19 pandemic highlighted the flexibility of devolved administrations in responding to local challenges. The crisis underscored the value of devolution in tailoring policies to meet the specific needs of different nations and regions within the UK.

The issue of Scottish independence remained a central theme in subsequent elections. The SNP's electoral successes demonstrated sustained support for the party's agenda. The UK government's handling of Brexit negotiations and its aftermath added fuel to the debate, with discussions about the potential impact of an independent Scotland on trade, economy, and international relations.

The changing political map of the UK, characterized by devolution and the rise of Scottish nationalism, highlighted the complexities of managing a diverse and evolving nation. The tension between the desire for greater autonomy and the aspiration for unity remained a challenge for policymakers and citizens alike. The story of devolution and the resurgence of Scottish nationalism is a reflection of the dynamic interplay between tradition and change, unity and diversity, and the ongoing evolution of the United Kingdom's political identity.

Multicultural Britain: Diversity, Immigration, and Identity

The story of modern Britain is inseparable from the narrative of multiculturalism—a journey shaped by waves of immigration, evolving cultural landscapes, and the quest to navigate the complexities of a diverse society. As the 20th and 21st centuries unfolded, Britain's identity transformed, reflecting the myriad influences that enriched its social fabric.

The post-World War II era marked a significant turning point in immigration patterns. The UK faced labor shortages and sought workers from former colonies, particularly the Caribbean, India, and Pakistan. The arrival of the "Windrush generation" from the Caribbean in 1948 laid the foundation for a multicultural society, with individuals contributing to the nation's recovery and development.

The 1960s saw an expansion of immigration as a result of changing global dynamics. South Asian communities, particularly from India, Bangladesh, and Pakistan, settled in the UK. These communities established vibrant cultural enclaves and contributed to the economic and social fabric of the nation.

In the latter half of the 20th century, immigration also included refugees and asylum seekers from conflict-affected regions such as Eastern Europe, the Middle East, and Africa. These migrations brought individuals seeking safety and new opportunities, further diversifying British society.

While immigration enriched British culture, it also prompted debates about identity, integration, and social cohesion. The notion of a "melting pot" versus a "multicultural mosaic" sparked discussions about the best approach to fostering unity while celebrating diversity.

Cultural expression flourished amidst this diverse tapestry. Restaurants offering international cuisines became a hallmark of British cities, reflecting the fusion of global flavors. Festivals, religious celebrations, and cultural events showcased the richness of different traditions, contributing to a shared sense of community.

However, the journey towards multiculturalism was not without challenges. Instances of racism, discrimination, and social exclusion persisted. The 1981 Brixton riots, driven by racial tensions and police-community conflicts, highlighted the need for greater understanding and integration.

Efforts to address these challenges included policies promoting equal rights and opportunities. The Race Relations Acts of 1965 and 1976 aimed to combat racial discrimination and promote social harmony. Organizations advocating for minority rights, such as the Runnymede Trust, played a role in advancing social change.

Education also played a pivotal role in shaping attitudes towards diversity. Schools embraced curricula that celebrated different cultures and histories, fostering a sense of belonging for young people from diverse backgrounds.

The incorporation of multicultural perspectives aimed to challenge biases and promote tolerance.

The legacy of multiculturalism continues to evolve in the 21st century. The 2001 census revealed that around 7.9 million people in the UK identified as belonging to an ethnic minority group. The increased visibility of minority communities and their contributions reshaped public discourse on race, identity, and representation.

Technological advancements and globalization further transformed multiculturalism. The internet facilitated connections between diverse communities, enabling the exchange of ideas and cultural practices. Social media provided platforms for individuals to share their stories and challenge stereotypes.

Brexit, the UK's decision to leave the European Union, raised questions about the impact on immigration and multiculturalism. Debates about immigration policy, citizenship, and the rights of EU citizens reflected differing visions of Britain's future.

The story of multicultural Britain is one of resilience, adaptation, and ongoing dialogue. It reflects a society in constant motion, embracing the challenges and opportunities that arise from its diversity. The journey towards multiculturalism exemplifies the power of coexistence, mutual respect, and understanding as the foundation for a more inclusive and harmonious nation.

Brexit and European Relations: Navigating a Complex Exit

The decision by the United Kingdom to leave the European Union, commonly referred to as Brexit, marked a historic and complex turning point in the nation's history. The process of disentangling from the EU and renegotiating relationships with European partners showcased the intricate challenges of untangling decades of political, economic, and social integration.

The journey towards Brexit was set in motion with the June 2016 referendum, in which 51.9% of voters chose to leave the EU. The decision had profound implications for the UK's relationship with its European neighbors, as well as for its domestic politics, economy, and international standing.

The negotiations that followed Brexit were a Herculean task, requiring agreements on issues ranging from trade to security cooperation. The key challenge was finding a balance between maintaining a close relationship with the EU while regaining national sovereignty—a delicate dance that would shape the terms of the exit.

One of the most contentious aspects of the negotiations was the question of the Irish border. The Good Friday Agreement of 1998 had brought peace to Northern Ireland, but the border issue threatened to reignite tensions. The need to prevent a hard border between Northern Ireland and the Republic of Ireland, while also respecting the integrity of the UK, posed a complex challenge.

The triggering of Article 50 in March 2017 officially initiated the process of leaving the EU. A period of intense negotiations ensued, with both the UK and the EU seeking to secure their interests and maintain stability. The negotiations were marked by debates over trade agreements, the rights of EU citizens in the UK, and the financial settlement known as the "divorce bill."

Prime Minister Theresa May's attempts to garner parliamentary support for a negotiated deal were met with challenges, leading to resignations from her cabinet and a lack of consensus within her own party. The uncertainty surrounding Brexit negotiations created economic volatility and heightened concerns about the potential consequences of a no-deal scenario.

The Withdrawal Agreement was eventually reached in November 2018, outlining the terms of the UK's exit from the EU. The agreement addressed citizens' rights, the financial settlement, and the transitional period to provide stability while a future trade relationship was negotiated.

However, the complexities of Brexit were far from over. The UK Parliament's rejection of the Withdrawal Agreement multiple times led to a series of extensions of the deadline for leaving the EU. The internal political divisions within the UK underscored the challenges of finding a path forward that would command broad support.

The situation took a new turn with the resignation of Theresa May as Prime Minister and the election of Boris Johnson in July 2019. Johnson advocated for a more assertive approach, pledging to renegotiate the Withdrawal Agreement and emphasizing a "do or die" commitment to leaving the EU by the new deadline of October 31, 2019.

In October 2019, a revised version of the Withdrawal Agreement was agreed upon between the UK and the EU. The agreement included changes to the Northern Ireland Protocol, aiming to avoid a hard border on the island of Ireland. Despite the new agreement, the UK faced further extensions and uncertainties, particularly in relation to the ongoing negotiations on future trade arrangements.

The year 2020 brought additional challenges in the form of the COVID-19 pandemic, further impacting negotiations and diverting attention and resources. Amid the pandemic, the UK formally left the EU on January 31, 2020, entering a transitional period during which the existing EU rules and regulations continued to apply.

The end of the transitional period on December 31, 2020, marked the complete departure of the UK from the EU's single market and customs union. The UK and the EU had reached a new trade agreement, but the changes in trading arrangements led to adjustments in various sectors, from customs procedures to regulations.

The impact of Brexit on various aspects of British life was substantial. Industries such as fisheries, agriculture, and manufacturing faced changes in trade rules and regulations. The UK's financial services sector also encountered shifts in its relationship with the EU, affecting access to European markets.

Brexit also prompted discussions about the UK's role in the international arena. As the UK sought to establish new trade relationships beyond the EU, it faced both opportunities and challenges in forging global partnerships. The UK's stance on issues such as climate change, security, and diplomacy continued to shape its relations with European partners.

The full implications of Brexit are still unfolding, and its impact on the UK's economy, society, and politics will continue to be a topic of study and debate. The story of Brexit highlights the complexities of disentangling from a complex political union and navigating the challenges of forging new relationships while preserving national interests and values.

Ancient Landscapes and Wildlife: Nature's History Across the Ages

The history of the United Kingdom's landscapes and wildlife stretches back millennia, shaped by geological forces, climatic shifts, and the interplay of various species. From the earliest formations of land to the diverse ecosystems that exist today, the story of nature's evolution across the ages is a testament to the intricate dance between time, environment, and life.

The ancient landscapes of the UK bear the imprints of tectonic movements that sculpted the land over millions of years. The geological history is rich, with evidence of volcanic activity, folding, and faulting that gave rise to mountain ranges, valleys, and coastlines. The iconic landscapes of the Scottish Highlands and the Lake District, for instance, are a result of these geological processes.

During the Ice Ages, which encompassed several periods of glaciation, ice sheets covered significant portions of the UK. The advancing and retreating ice sculpted the land, leaving behind features such as U-shaped valleys and moraines. As the climate warmed, these glaciers receded, revealing the modern topography that we see today.

The UK's ancient landscapes are home to a diverse range of wildlife, both past and present. Fossil records provide insights into the prehistoric inhabitants of the region. Mammoths, giant deer, and woolly rhinoceroses roamed the land during the Pleistocene epoch, adapting to the challenges of changing climates.

As the Ice Ages waned and the climate stabilized, temperate forests dominated the landscape. Ancient woodlands, such as the Caledonian Forest in Scotland, have survived for thousands of years, offering a glimpse into the ecosystems of the past. These woodlands were home to a variety of wildlife, including wolves, wild boars, and red deer.

The arrival of human communities marked a significant shift in the relationship between people and the environment. Early inhabitants engaged in hunting, gathering, and later, agriculture. Ancient monuments, such as Stonehenge, offer tantalizing hints about the spiritual significance of the natural world to these early societies.

Medieval landscapes were shaped by the expansion of human settlements and agriculture. Forests were cleared, marshes were drained, and fields were cultivated. This transformation led to the creation of distinct habitats and the coexistence of humans with wildlife such as rabbits, foxes, and various bird species.

The Industrial Revolution brought unprecedented changes to the landscape. Urbanization, industrialization, and the growth of transportation networks led to alterations in land use and the encroachment on natural habitats. Wildlife faced new challenges as habitats were fragmented and polluted.

Conservation efforts began to gain traction in the 19th and 20th centuries in response to concerns about declining wildlife populations and habitat loss. The establishment of nature reserves, such as the RSPB's Minsmere in Suffolk, aimed to protect and restore habitats for native species.

Efforts were also made to reintroduce species that had become locally extinct, such as the red kite and the beaver.

The UK's landscapes and wildlife continue to face challenges in the modern era. Urbanization, agricultural intensification, climate change, and invasive species impact the delicate balance of ecosystems. Conservation initiatives aim to address these challenges and promote sustainable coexistence between humans and nature.

In recent years, there has been a growing recognition of the value of rewilding—allowing nature to restore itself through natural processes. Rewilding projects, such as the reintroduction of beavers to help manage water systems and improve habitats, highlight the potential for humans to work in harmony with nature.

The story of the UK's ancient landscapes and wildlife is one of resilience, adaptation, and interconnectedness. It is a tale of geological forces shaping the land, of prehistoric creatures navigating changing environments, of human societies interacting with their surroundings, and of modern conservation efforts striving to preserve the natural world for future generations.

Culinary Journey Through Time: From Tudor Banquets to Modern Cuisine

The culinary history of the United Kingdom is a captivating journey that reflects the evolution of tastes, traditions, and techniques over the centuries. From extravagant Tudor banquets to the fusion of global flavors in modern cuisine, the story of food in the UK provides a window into the cultural, social, and economic changes that have shaped the nation.

In the Tudor period, elaborate feasts were a hallmark of the royal court and aristocratic households. The rich and powerful showcased their status through opulent banquets featuring roasted meats, game birds, and lavish displays of sugar sculptures. Spices imported from distant lands, such as cinnamon and nutmeg, were prized for their exotic allure.

The arrival of sugar in the 16th century marked a transformation in culinary practices. Sweet treats, once reserved for the elite, became more accessible to a broader range of people. Sugar was incorporated into a variety of dishes, from custards and tarts to sweetened beverages.

The influence of trade and exploration introduced new ingredients to British kitchens. The 17th century saw the introduction of potatoes, tomatoes, and tea, which would eventually become staples of British cuisine. The popularity of tea, imported from China and later India, led to the development of the British tradition of afternoon tea.

The Industrial Revolution brought significant changes to the way people ate. Urbanization and the growth of factory work prompted the need for quick and convenient meals. Street food vendors offered affordable options such as meat pies and fish and chips, which quickly became popular among the working class.

The Victorian era witnessed a shift towards more formal dining etiquette and elaborate dinner parties. The emergence of cookbooks and household manuals provided guidance on proper table settings, meal planning, and culinary techniques. The first celebrity chefs, such as Alexis Soyer, gained recognition for their culinary expertise.

The late 19th and early 20th centuries brought the influence of foreign cuisines to the UK. Indian, Chinese, and Middle Eastern flavors began to appear on British menus, reflecting the nation's colonial connections and growing interest in international cuisine. The establishment of curry houses in the UK marked the beginning of the nation's love affair with curry.

The rationing and food shortages of World War I and World War II led to a period of culinary innovation and adaptation. Home cooks were forced to be creative with limited resources, leading to the invention of dishes such as the "wartime loaf" and "mock apple pie" made from crackers.

In the post-war period, a more cosmopolitan culinary landscape emerged. The 1960s and 70s witnessed a surge of interest in continental European cuisine, with French and Italian dishes becoming popular choices. The 1980s saw a renewed focus on British ingredients and traditional recipes, led by chefs like Fergus Henderson and his "nose-to-tail" philosophy.

The 21st century brought a culinary renaissance characterized by innovation, fusion, and a celebration of local produce. Renowned chefs like Heston Blumenthal pushed the boundaries of gastronomy with experimental techniques and whimsical presentations. The farm-to-table movement gained traction, emphasizing sustainability and the importance of seasonal ingredients.

The UK's diverse population also contributed to the multicultural flavors of modern British cuisine. The fusion of global influences has given rise to dishes such as chicken tikka masala, hailed by many as a British national dish.

The rise of food media, cooking shows, and celebrity chefs has further elevated the importance of food in British culture. Food festivals, farmers' markets, and gourmet dining experiences have become integral parts of the culinary landscape.

The journey through time reveals the remarkable evolution of British cuisine, from Tudor banquets to the eclectic fusion of flavors seen today. Each era has left its mark, shaping not only the way people eat but also the way they gather, celebrate, and express their identities through food.

Iconic Landmarks and Historic Sites: Tracing Footsteps of the Past

The United Kingdom's landscape is dotted with iconic landmarks and historic sites that stand as testaments to the nation's rich history, culture, and heritage. From prehistoric stone circles to grand castles, from magnificent cathedrals to bustling city streets, these landmarks offer a glimpse into the footsteps of the past, inviting visitors to explore the stories they hold.

One of the most enduring and enigmatic landmarks is Stonehenge, a Neolithic stone circle located on Salisbury Plain. Dating back over 4,000 years, Stonehenge has captivated the imagination of generations. Its purpose, construction methods, and alignment with celestial events continue to be subjects of study and speculation.

The Tower of London, with its centuries of history and imposing presence, is another iconic landmark. Originally built as a royal palace and later serving as a prison and treasury, the Tower has witnessed events ranging from coronations to executions. The Crown Jewels are housed within its walls, symbolizing the monarchy's enduring role.

Westminster Abbey, a masterpiece of Gothic architecture, has hosted numerous coronations, royal weddings, and burials of historical figures. The Abbey's intricate stonework, stained glass windows, and rich history make it a place of reverence and reflection.

The Palace of Westminster, often referred to as the Houses of Parliament, is home to the UK's political heart. The iconic clock tower, known as Big Ben (now the Elizabeth Tower), has become a symbol of London and British democracy.

Edinburgh Castle, perched atop an ancient volcanic hill, dominates the skyline of Scotland's capital city. Its origins trace back to the Iron Age, and it has played a crucial role in Scotland's history, from royal residence to military stronghold.

The Roman Baths in Bath, a UNESCO World Heritage site, offer a glimpse into the opulent lifestyles of ancient Roman Britain. The well-preserved ruins include bathing and temple complexes, showcasing the engineering marvels of the time.

Hadrian's Wall, stretching across northern England, was built by the Romans to mark the northern boundary of their empire. The wall's remnants stand as a reminder of the Roman presence and the complexities of border control even in ancient times.

The historic city of Oxford, with its "dreaming spires," is home to the University of Oxford, one of the oldest and most prestigious universities in the world. The university's colleges, libraries, and museums reflect centuries of scholarly pursuits.

Stratford-upon-Avon, the birthplace of William Shakespeare, draws visitors from around the globe to explore the playwright's legacy. His birthplace, Anne Hathaway's Cottage, and the Royal Shakespeare Theatre pay homage to his enduring influence.

The Giant's Causeway in Northern Ireland, a natural wonder of interlocking hexagonal basalt columns, is steeped in myth and legend. Formed by volcanic activity, the site's unique formations have inspired stories for centuries.

The historic city of Bath is known for its Georgian architecture, thermal springs, and the elegant Bath Abbey. The city's Roman Baths and Pump Room offer a glimpse into its spa town past.

From the medieval majesty of York Minster to the prehistoric intrigue of Avebury's stone circle, the United Kingdom's landmarks and historic sites offer a kaleidoscope of history, architecture, and cultural heritage. These sites weave together a narrative that spans millennia, inviting visitors to step into the past and gain a deeper appreciation for the layers of history that have shaped the nation.

London: From Roman Londinium to Global Metropolis

The city of London, a dynamic and diverse metropolis, has a history that spans over two thousand years, making it one of the world's oldest continuously inhabited cities. From its humble beginnings as a Roman settlement to its current status as a global financial and cultural hub, London's journey is a reflection of human progress, resilience, and evolution.

London's story begins with its establishment as a Roman settlement named Londinium around 43 AD. Located along the banks of the River Thames, Londinium served as a key trading and transportation hub within the Roman province of Britannia. The city's strategic location allowed it to grow rapidly, with a bustling port and an array of markets and public buildings.

The Romans built the London Wall, a defensive fortification, around Londinium in the late 2nd century. Parts of this wall can still be seen today, offering a glimpse into the city's ancient past. The Romans also constructed the Roman amphitheater, a site where gladiatorial contests and other forms of entertainment took place.

The decline of the Roman Empire led to Londinium's abandonment in the early 5th century. However, the city's importance persisted, as Anglo-Saxon settlements emerged in the area. The establishment of Westminster Abbey in the 7th century marked the beginning of London's association with English royalty and governance.

The medieval period saw London grow as a trading center, with the Tower of London serving as a royal palace, fortress, and treasury. The city's connection to trade routes led to the establishment of guilds and the growth of a merchant class. The construction of London Bridge, a stone bridge across the Thames, further facilitated commerce and travel.

The Great Fire of London in 1666 caused widespread destruction, leading to a significant rebuilding effort. Renowned architect Christopher Wren played a pivotal role in redesigning the city's churches, including the iconic St. Paul's Cathedral. The city's architectural landscape began to reflect a blend of historic and modern influences.

The 18th and 19th centuries saw London's expansion and transformation into a global center of commerce, culture, and innovation. The Industrial Revolution brought rapid urbanization, with new industries and technologies changing the face of the city. London's role as an imperial capital facilitated the exchange of ideas and goods from around the world.

The Victorian era left an indelible mark on London's infrastructure and architecture. The construction of railway stations, including Paddington and King's Cross, revolutionized transportation. The iconic red-brick terraced houses, often associated with London, became emblematic of the city's urban landscape.

London's cultural scene flourished during the 20th century. The city's theaters, galleries, and music venues showcased artistic innovation and creativity. The West End became synonymous with world-class theater productions, while the birth of punk rock in the 1970s added a rebellious edge to the city's musical legacy.

The 21st century has witnessed London's continued growth as a global metropolis. The city's financial district, known as the Square Mile, is a hub for international finance and commerce. Modern skyscrapers, such as The Shard and the Walkie-Talkie building, now dominate the skyline.

London's cultural diversity is a defining feature of its modern identity. The city is a melting pot of cultures, languages, and cuisines, with neighborhoods like Chinatown, Brick Lane, and Little India showcasing the richness of its multicultural tapestry.

From its origins as a Roman outpost to its current status as a vibrant and cosmopolitan city, London's journey has been shaped by countless generations, each leaving their mark on its landscape and character. The resilience, innovation, and adaptability that have defined London's history continue to make it a place of fascination and inspiration for people from all corners of the globe.

Edinburgh: Capital of Scotland's Heritage and Innovation

Nestled between rugged hills and overlooking the North Sea, Edinburgh stands as a city of remarkable contrasts, where history and innovation intertwine to create a unique tapestry. As the capital of Scotland, Edinburgh boasts a rich heritage that spans centuries, while also serving as a hub of creativity and progress that has left an indelible mark on the world.

The roots of Edinburgh's history date back to the ancient past. The city's foundations can be traced to the early Middle Ages, when it emerged as a prominent settlement atop Castle Rock. Edinburgh Castle, perched atop this volcanic formation, played a pivotal role in the city's development, evolving from a fortress to a royal residence.

The Old Town, a labyrinthine network of narrow streets and alleyways, preserves the city's medieval layout. The Royal Mile, a historic thoroughfare that stretches from the Castle to the Palace of Holyroodhouse, encapsulates Edinburgh's past with its well-preserved architecture and centuries-old buildings.

In the 18th century, Edinburgh experienced a period of intellectual enlightenment known as the Scottish Enlightenment. The city's coffeehouses and salons became gathering places for philosophers, writers, and scientists who exchanged ideas that would shape the world. Figures like David Hume, Adam Smith, and James Hutton contributed to advancements in philosophy, economics, and geology.

The New Town, a contrast to the Old Town's winding alleys, was designed in the late 18th century with grand neoclassical architecture, wide streets, and spacious squares. This urban expansion was not just about aesthetics; it embodied the city's embrace of modernity and its aspiration to be a thriving center of commerce and culture.

Edinburgh's literary legacy is a source of pride. Sir Walter Scott, often referred to as the "Wizard of the North," penned works that continue to captivate readers. His historical novels, including "Ivanhoe" and "Waverley," showcased the city's history and landscapes, contributing to the Romantic movement.

The city's cultural vibrancy is celebrated annually during the Edinburgh Festival Fringe, the world's largest arts festival. Every August, artists and performers from across the globe descend upon the city, transforming it into a stage for theater, music, comedy, and visual arts. The festival's inclusivity and boundary-pushing ethos have made it a hallmark of artistic expression.

Edinburgh's architectural marvels extend beyond its historic and neoclassical buildings. The Scottish Parliament Building, designed by Enric Miralles, is a modern masterpiece that reflects the aspirations of a devolved Scotland. Its innovative design symbolizes the city's commitment to progress and self-governance.

The city's academic prowess is anchored by the University of Edinburgh, one of the oldest universities in the English-speaking world. Its influence on scientific discovery is exemplified by alumni like Charles Darwin and Alexander Graham Bell, whose groundbreaking work in evolution and communication revolutionized the world.

Edinburgh's cultural heritage is preserved within its museums and galleries. The National Museum of Scotland showcases the country's history, from prehistoric artifacts to contemporary art. The Scottish National Gallery, on the other hand, houses an impressive collection of European masterpieces.

The city's role as a center of innovation continues to thrive. Edinburgh's burgeoning tech scene, often referred to as the "Silicon Glen," is a hotbed of technological advancements and startups. This convergence of history and technology echoes the city's tradition of embracing change while honoring its heritage.

As the capital of Scotland, Edinburgh has witnessed the evolution of a nation and contributed to global progress. Its heritage, creativity, and innovations stand as a testament to the human spirit's ability to adapt, create, and shape the world. From its medieval alleys to its modern skylines, Edinburgh remains a city that bridges the past and the future in a captivating embrace.

Cardiff to Belfast: Capitals of Changing Nations

The capitals of Wales and Northern Ireland, Cardiff and Belfast, each carry a unique narrative of cultural, political, and societal transformations. These cities serve as microcosms of their respective nations, reflecting the complex histories that have shaped their identities and trajectories.

Cardiff: A Welsh Metamorphosis

Cardiff, the capital of Wales, has undergone a remarkable evolution from its humble origins to its present status as a thriving and diverse urban center. Its history is deeply intertwined with Wales' struggles for recognition, identity, and autonomy.

Founded as a Roman fort, Cardiff's strategic location along the River Taff made it a crucial hub for trade and commerce. The Norman Conquest of Wales in the 11th century led to the construction of Cardiff Castle, a symbol of Norman rule. Over time, the city became a key player in the coal industry, transforming into a global coal-exporting hub during the Industrial Revolution.

The 20th century marked a turning point for Cardiff as the capital of Wales. The establishment of the Welsh Office in the city in 1964 marked a step towards devolution and recognition of Welsh identity. The National Assembly for Wales, later renamed the Senedd, was established in

Cardiff Bay in 1999, granting Wales a degree of legislative power.

Cardiff's urban landscape reflects its journey. The rejuvenation of Cardiff Bay, once an industrial port, has transformed it into a modern waterfront district. Iconic landmarks like the Wales Millennium Centre and the Senedd stand as testaments to the nation's cultural and political aspirations.

Belfast: A City of Shifting Landscapes

Belfast, the capital of Northern Ireland, has grappled with a complex history that transcends its role as a political and economic hub. Its story is shaped by the dualities of identity, conflict, and reconciliation that characterize Northern Ireland's narrative.

Belfast's origins can be traced back to its establishment as a medieval settlement, which grew into a thriving industrial city during the 19th century. Shipbuilding, linen production, and the famed Harland and Wolff shipyards contributed to Belfast's economic prominence. However, the city's history is also marked by sectarian tensions between its Protestant and Catholic communities.

The Troubles, a period of violent conflict between nationalist and unionist factions, left an indelible mark on Belfast. The city was deeply divided, with the Peace Walls still standing as physical manifestations of these divisions. The Good Friday Agreement in 1998 marked a pivotal moment of hope and reconciliation, leading to relative stability and the slow process of dismantling barriers.

Belfast's revival in the 21st century is a testament to its resilience. The waterfront Titanic Quarter, named after the famous ship built in the city, is now a symbol of urban regeneration and cultural renaissance. Museums, galleries, and cultural festivals contribute to Belfast's image as a vibrant and forward-looking capital.

Changing Nations, Enduring Capitals

Both Cardiff and Belfast are capitals that have navigated complex transitions. As political landscapes shift, these cities remain focal points of identity and aspiration for their respective nations. Their histories reveal the interconnectedness of local and national narratives, reflecting the intricate interplay of culture, politics, and progress.

Oxford and Cambridge: Centers of Scholarly Excellence

The universities of Oxford and Cambridge, often collectively referred to as Oxbridge, stand as iconic symbols of academic prestige and intellectual rigor. These institutions have played an integral role in shaping the intellectual landscape of not only the United Kingdom but also the world, fostering generations of scholars, scientists, thinkers, and leaders.

Oxford: A Tapestry of Knowledge

Oxford University, located in the historic city of Oxford, traces its origins back to the 12th century. Its storied history is interwoven with the rise of medieval learning and the pursuit of knowledge in an era marked by intellectual curiosity.

The university's collegiate structure sets it apart. Over 30 self-governing colleges, each with its own character and history, create a rich tapestry of academic life. These colleges provide students with a close-knit community, fostering an environment where interdisciplinary exchange and intellectual exploration thrive.

Oxford's academic legacy is a constellation of luminaries. The likes of J.R.R. Tolkien, C.S. Lewis, Stephen Hawking, and countless others have graced its halls. Its libraries, such as the Bodleian Library, house an impressive collection of manuscripts and texts that span centuries, reflecting the depth of scholarly pursuit.

Cambridge: A Beacon of Innovation

Cambridge University, located in the city of Cambridge, shares a similar origin, tracing its roots to the 13th century. It has cultivated a reputation for innovation and groundbreaking research across disciplines.

The university's scientific contributions are immeasurable. Sir Isaac Newton's groundbreaking work on gravity and optics revolutionized the understanding of the natural world. The discovery of the structure of DNA by James Watson and Francis Crick marked a turning point in the field of genetics.

Cambridge's collaborative culture fosters academic curiosity. The "Cambridge Phenomenon," an influx of tech companies and startups in the 20th century, led to the establishment of the so-called "Silicon Fen." This innovation hub reflects the university's role in shaping not just academic thought but also technological advancement.

Excellence in Diversity

Both Oxford and Cambridge have embraced diversity over time. These institutions have made strides in promoting access and inclusion, though challenges remain. Efforts to increase diversity in admissions and address historical inequalities reflect their commitment to being institutions that reflect the broader society they serve.

Oxbridge: A Global Influence

The impact of Oxbridge extends beyond national borders. The influence of its scholars, research, and academic traditions is felt across continents. Graduates of these universities have gone on to shape fields as diverse as literature, politics, science, and the arts, leaving an indelible mark on the global intellectual landscape.

Enduring Excellence

Oxford and Cambridge continue to be beacons of scholarly excellence. Their legacy, shaped by centuries of inquiry and innovation, demonstrates the power of education to propel humanity forward. These universities remain vibrant, dynamic, and adaptable institutions that stand as pillars of knowledge, creativity, and progress.

Mysteries of Stonehenge: Unveiling the Enigma of Ancient Britain

The enigmatic monument of Stonehenge stands as one of the most iconic symbols of ancient Britain, captivating the imagination of generations with its imposing stone circle and enigmatic purpose. Situated on Salisbury Plain in Wiltshire, this prehistoric site has intrigued archaeologists, historians, and visitors alike, sparking numerous theories and speculations about its origin, construction, and significance.

Stonehenge's origins can be traced back to around 3000 BCE during the late Neolithic period. The monument evolved over centuries, with its final form consisting of a circular arrangement of massive upright stones, known as sarsens, topped by horizontal lintels. Inner circles of smaller bluestones were later added, creating a layered architectural composition.

The construction of Stonehenge was a remarkable feat of engineering for its time. The transportation of the massive sarsen stones, some weighing up to 30 tons, from a quarry nearly 20 miles away remains a puzzle. Theories suggest that a combination of sledges, rollers, and possibly water transportation was employed to move these colossal stones.

One of the enduring mysteries surrounding Stonehenge is its alignment with celestial events. The monument's layout appears to be astronomically significant, with the central axis aligning with the sunrise during the summer solstice and the sunset during the winter solstice. This suggests a potential connection to rituals or ceremonies linked to solar and lunar cycles.

Stonehenge's purpose remains a subject of speculation. Many theories propose that it was a site of religious or spiritual significance, possibly serving as a place for rituals, ceremonies, and worship. The alignment with solstices and equinoxes suggests an observatory-like function for tracking celestial events.

Another theory proposes Stonehenge as a center for healing and medicine. The bluestones that make up part of the monument are believed to have been transported from Wales, a considerable distance. The bluestones have been linked to the concept of healing due to their believed mystical properties.

The people who built Stonehenge left behind no written records, contributing to the mystery surrounding its purpose. However, recent archaeological research has shed light on the people who erected the monument. They were likely a Neolithic community with a deep connection to the land and a belief in the importance of ancestors and lineage.

Stonehenge's significance as a World Heritage Site has led to efforts to preserve and study the monument. Excavations, laser scans, and archaeological research have offered insights into its construction techniques, the source of its stones, and potential human activity around the site.

Despite extensive research, Stonehenge's purpose remains a tantalizing mystery. The monument's legacy has left an enduring impact on art, literature, and popular culture. Its aura of mystique continues to draw visitors and researchers, sparking ongoing inquiries into the Neolithic mind, its relationship with the cosmos, and the rituals that may have been conducted within its stone circle.

Stonehenge stands as an emblem of human ingenuity and curiosity. As archaeologists and scientists strive to unlock its secrets, the monument remains an enduring reminder of the deep connections between ancient societies and the natural world. The mysteries of Stonehenge invite contemplation, encouraging us to look back in time and ponder the complex narrative of ancient Britain.

Conclusion

The history of the United Kingdom is a tapestry woven from the threads of time, intricately blending ancient legacies with modern innovations. From its earliest inhabitants who left their mark on the landscape to the dynamic cities that bear the imprints of centuries, the UK's journey is one of resilience, evolution, and transformation.

Across the chapters of this book, we have traversed through the annals of time, exploring the rise and fall of kingdoms, the clashes of ideologies, and the indomitable spirit of a nation. We've delved into the stories of rulers and rebels, visionaries and inventors, each leaving an indelible mark on the fabric of British history.

From the ancient landscapes of Stonehenge to the bustling metropolises of London, Edinburgh, Cardiff, and Belfast, we've witnessed the ebb and flow of culture, politics, and society. The UK's historical narrative is as diverse as its people, reflecting the complexities and contradictions inherent in any nation's journey.

Through triumphs and tribulations, the UK has navigated the challenges of warfare, colonization, and societal upheaval. It has been a crucible of creativity, birthing literary giants, scientific pioneers, and cultural revolutions that reverberate far beyond its shores.

In this modern age, the UK stands as a global player, bearing the imprints of its rich history while embracing the opportunities and challenges of the 21st century. The echoes of its past continue to shape its present, with each step forward rooted in a deep understanding of the forces that have shaped its path.

As we close this chapter, it's evident that the story of the United Kingdom is an ongoing narrative, a living testament to the resilience, adaptability, and creativity of its people. The legacy of the past merges seamlessly with the aspirations of the future, creating a nation that stands at the crossroads of tradition and progress, heritage and innovation.

The history of the United Kingdom is a reminder that the human experience is a complex interplay of individual actions and collective destinies. It is a story that invites reflection, exploration, and a deeper understanding of the forces that have shaped a nation and its place in the world.

We hope you've enjoyed this journey through the captivating history of the United Kingdom. From ancient civilizations to modern transformations, the story of the UK is one of resilience, innovation, and the interplay of diverse cultures.

Your interest in exploring these chapters has allowed us to share this rich tapestry of the past, and we're truly grateful for your time and attention. If this book has enriched your understanding and sparked your curiosity, we kindly ask you to consider leaving a positive review. Your feedback is invaluable and will help others discover the fascinating history of the United Kingdom.

Once again, thank you for being part of this exploration. We look forward to continuing to provide you with engaging and informative content.

Manufactured by Amazon.ca
Acheson, AB

11303001R00070